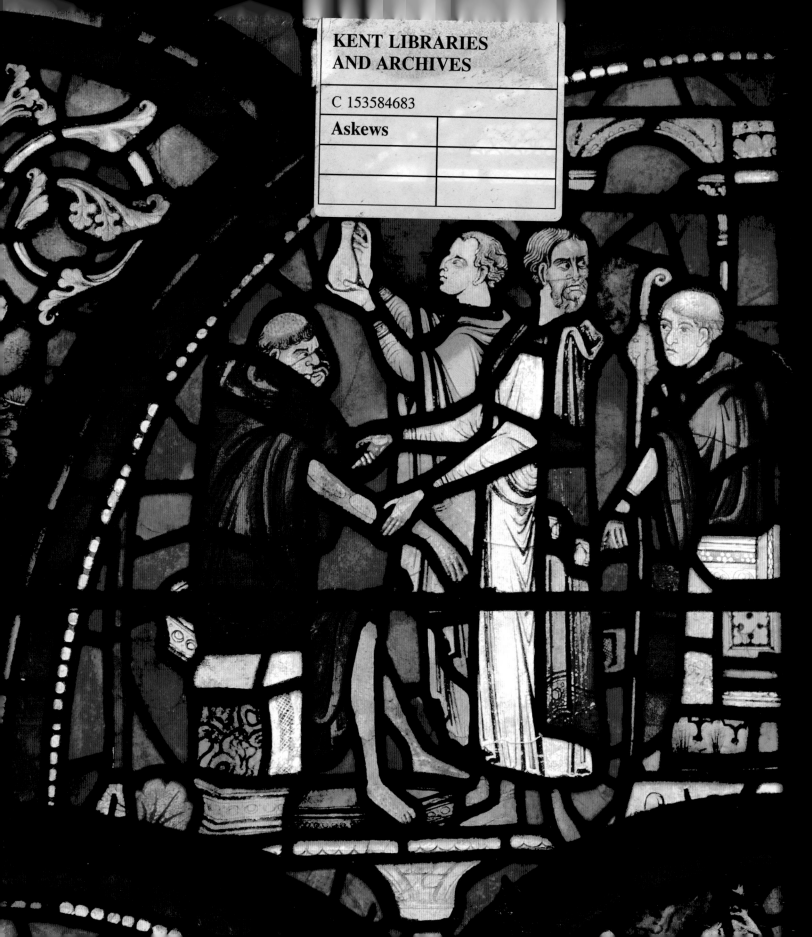

Painton Cowen

English Stained Glass

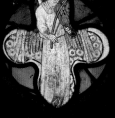

with 200 colour illustrations

Thames & Hudson

p. 1 East window, **Malvern Priory**, c. 1440

pp. 2–3 Detail from **Canterbury Cathedral**, c. 1220

p. 3 Detail from **St Mary the Virgin, Saxlingham Nethergate**, 15th century

First published in the United Kingdom in 2008 by Thames & Hudson Ltd,
181A High Holborn, London WC1V 7QX

www.thamesandhudson.com

© 2008 Thames & Hudson Ltd, London
All photographs, unless otherwise stated, © Painton Cowen

British Library Cataloguing-in-Publication Data
A catalogue record for this book is available from the British Library

ISBN 978-0-500-23846-2

Printed and bound in Singapore by C. S. Graphics

Contents

The numbers preceding place names below correspond with those on the map, left. Names of churches in **bold italic** indicate that they are the subject of a special feature.

Introduction: The Art of Light 8

East Anglia

The South and South-West

Introduction:
The Art of Light

Englsh stained glass inhabits a curious position within the study of the visual arts. For many years seen by scholars as having little artistic value, it tended to be of more interest to antiquarians who took delight in poring over the heraldry found in so much English glass. Yet at the same time, it has always been very popular with worshippers and visitors to churches, who have often found in it an immediate spiritual resonance. Indeed, at its best, English medieval glass helps bring to life the architecture of many venerable churches and cathedrals, big and small.

This book covers the golden age of stained glass in England – approximately from 1100 to 1530. That the production of stained glass continued throughout the medieval period is ample testament to its perceived importance in the decoration of churches. Of course, the period saw many changes in both style and content, which reflected changing architectural tastes as well as changes within the Church. Twelfth-century glass is radically different even to 14th-century glass in terms of colour, handling of the brush, arrangement of subject matter, size, shape and ornament; by the 16th century stained glass was largely imitating panel painting. In addition, the function of stained glass changes both with time but also according to the nature of the building and the intended audience. Close attention to stained glass is always rewarded, and hopefully this book gives some ideas as to how to read these windows.

Recent scholarship has shown that with the rapid adoption and evolution of stained glass in the 12th and 13th centuries the craft itself was responsible for many artistic innovations and traditions that spread into other media. However, while there may be superficial similarities to ivories, enamels, altarpiece carvings, sculpture, manuscript illumination and wall paintings, it should also be remembered that stained glass has its own language. Successful glass designs use the rhythms of the lead lines and the rich colours and painting technique that the medium affords to create a unique art form. The groupings and representations of people, the simplicity and economy of backgrounds and the pared-down and stylized props for the varying scenes all reflect this unique language.

While the finest stained glass in England easily ranks with that of any country on the Continent, in fact it may be anachronistic to draw boundaries since much of the glass was produced by glaziers from the Continent – earlier from France, later from the Low Countries or Germany. If such movement of artists naturally raises the question of what to feature in this book, the criterion for inclusion is that the glass was commissioned by English patrons for English churches. Even when produced by overseas workshops, glass tends to reflect local or national concerns, cults of saints (for example, Thomas Becket and Alphege at Canterbury, Edmund in Northumbria, Neot and Kew in Cornwall, and Frideswide in Oxford) and tastes (especially in the 14th century). That said, the fundamental subjects of stained glass – the Nativity, the Passion, the Last Judgment, as well as other Old and New Testament scenes – appear equally in English and Continental glass, and reflect the concerns of the Universal Church. Little secular glass survives, and that which does tends to be heraldic.

In addition to national styles and preoccupations, by the 15th century there are clearly defined regional schools of glass painters in England. For this reason the book is organized into four regions – *The North, The Midlands, East Anglia* and *The South and South-West* – which roughly reflect these schools. While every book is limited in space, I have taken care to choose the most distinctive and important pieces from each region, as well as including a few less well known personal favourites. It is hoped that this organization also shows that one doesn't have to travel very far to see something really special. As for whether stained glass counts as art, or mere decoration, it is hoped that the photographs will prove even more persuasive than words.

Previous spread **St Mary's Guildhall, Coventry.** This magnificent array of kings dates to c. 1451–61. From left to right we can see King Arthur, William I, Richard I, Henry III, Henry VI, Edward III, Henry IV, Henry V and Constantine.

The story of stained glass in England begins very early, with evidence of coloured window glass from the Anglo-Saxon period at Jarrow, Monkwearmouth (7th–9th centuries), and the Old Minster at Winchester (10th century), though these are only fragments. At this early stage windows were generally very small, and it seems certain that the glass would rarely have been figurative but instead very simply patterned. Bede tells us that at Monkwearmouth Abbot Benedict Biscop had to call upon French glaziers to furnish his church, suggesting that the craft was not yet well-developed in England. Such early survivals are extremely rare, however, and it is only from the late 11th century onwards that we find large stained glass windows anywhere in Europe. Broadly speaking, the large, figurative stained glass window is a Romanesque invention, tied to developments in architecture that resulted in larger window openings, as well as in an increasing emphasis on ornament.

Romanesque glass shares much stylistically and iconographically with sculpture of the period, and concentrates on single, hierarchic figures rather than trying to depict whole stories. A good example of this would be the figure of St Michael in the church of All Saints, Dalbury (Derbyshire), which probably dates from the first quarter of the 12th century (though it could be from the end of the previous century). Another popular subject in the mid-12th century was the Tree of Jesse, showing the ancestry of Christ. This was particularly suited to the ever taller and narrower lancet windows of the early Gothic style, which began to dominate from the 1140s onwards. Indeed, some scholars have even suggested that the transition from Romanesque to Gothic was actually driven by a desire to have larger panels of stained glass. At York Minster a single figure from a Tree of Jesse has survived that used to be dated as early as *c.* 1150 (though *c.* 1180 seems more likely). It bears certain stylistic resemblances to the Trees of Jesse at the abbey of St Denis (just outside Paris) and the cathedral of Chartres, also in France, which date, respectively, from 1144 and *c.* 1150. Other popular early subjects include the Last Judgment, and also typological scenes that show how events in the Old Testament prefigured those of the New Testament. Thus we often find a scene of the prophet Jonah emerging from the belly of the whale alongside one of the Resurrection, or of Abraham about to sacrifice Isaac next to the Crucifixion.

Probably the oldest complete figure panel of stained glass in Britain, at **All Saints, Dalbury**, Derbyshire. The Byzantine-inspired 'orans' position with the splayed hands, the large staring eyes and cloak pattern all suggest an early 12th-century date, possibly even late 11th century.

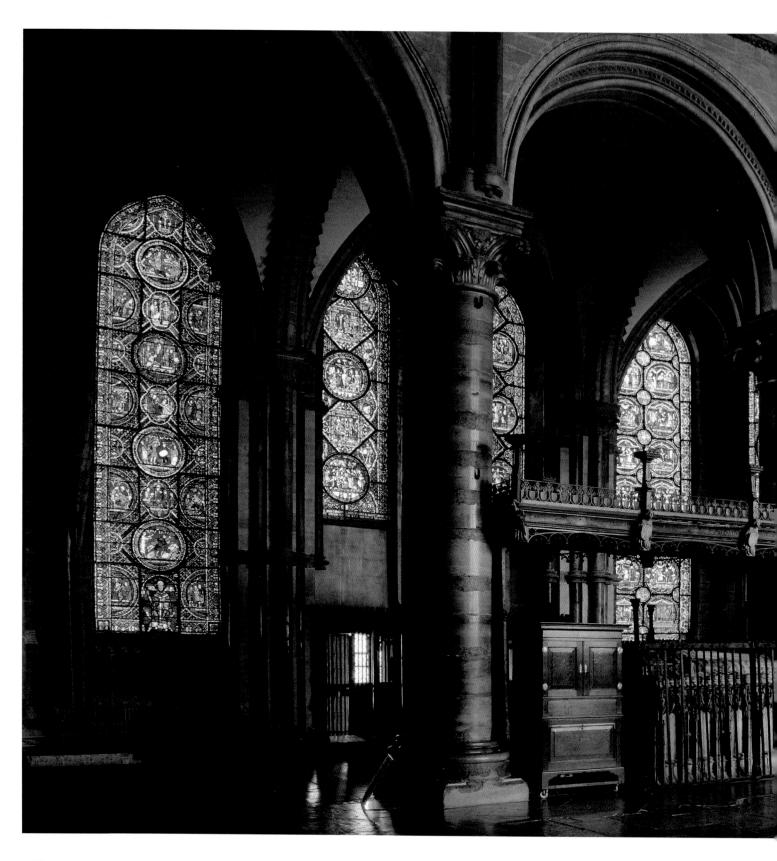

Such scenes appear at Canterbury Cathedral, which is the first important collection of stained glass in England. Some of the stately figures of the kings and prophets Rehoboam, David, Nathan and Abijah, originally in the choir clearstorey and now in the west window and south transept, are now thought to date from before the fire of 1174, and perhaps from as early as *c.* 1155–60. The other major monument, as already mentioned, is York Minster, the choir of which was built between 1154 and 1181. Some of this early choir glass commissioned by Archbishop Roger remains, though since restored and relocated within the church. Like Abbot Biscop in the 9th century, Archbishop Roger had to call on French glaziers for the windows. This was not too unusual, considering the political ties between the two countries in the 12th century, and indeed one of the principal architects of Canterbury, William of Sens, was also French. In time English styles were also exported back to France (for example, at Sens Cathedral).

By the beginning of the 13th century the craft of stained glass design and manufacture was practised on a considerable scale, supplying hundreds of abbeys, churches and cathedrals throughout England. Already the craft was organized into workshops or *ateliers* with a master presiding, although few names can be put to specific installations before the 13th century. Glassmakers, glaziers and their workshops could be found in York, Canterbury, Lincoln, Westminster, Coventry, Bath, Norwich, Oxford and Chester, as well as at numerous abbeys. Although we may not have names, we can sometimes discern a particular individual's hand at work from window to window (as at Canterbury) and even, on occasion, from site to site.

The year 1200 saw widespread building of churches and cathedrals throughout Europe in the High Gothic style, with great emphasis placed on the size of the windows. Throughout the 12th century glass painting had developed alongside other arts including wall painting and sculpture, and the churches of around 1200 often have sophisticated iconographic programmes that unite these different media. One important development

Trinity Chapel, Canterbury Cathedral. After the murder of Becket in 1170 his cult grew rapidly, and this shrine was built by 1220. The surrounding windows recount in stained glass the miracles associated with him, but at the same time infuse the space with coloured light, evoking the sparkling jewels of the Heavenly Jerusalem. Early pilgrims to the shrine at Canterbury must have been astonished.

How a Window is Made

The process of making a window changed little over the medieval period. The first step was to decide what was to be depicted. Donor, glazier and the church authorities would have agreed upon a subject and position in the building, initially using a sketch or *vidimus*. Once agreed, a full-size cartoon was drawn on a tabletop covered with whitewash. Since the different coloured glasses have to be joined by pieces of lead this cartoon marked the outline of the design based on the lead lines within each panel. Each colour in the design would have been annotated with a symbol and the painting to be added to the glass indicated. Such a design could be used again and again with variations in painting and colours to give a different figure (both Tewkesbury Abbey and Gloucester Cathedral have good examples of this).

Glass-making and glazing were separate professions, carried out in different locations. Our best idea today of both processes comes from the 12th-century German Benedictine monk Theophilus's *De Diversis Artibus*. Coloured glass generally came from the Continent, particularly Normandy and the Lorraine–Flanders region, though some 'white' (clear) glass was manufactured in England, particularly in the Surrey and Sussex areas. The basic constituents of glass are silica (found in river sand) and wood ash, to which are added small quantities of particular metal oxides for coloration. Copper oxide produces green, red and turquoise blue; manganese a fairly consistent violet colour; iron gives yellow, green and varieties of blue, as well as a kind of red. Cobalt gives a particular kind of blue, chrome the most common green, while nickel is another multicolour oxide giving violet, brown or even another kind of blue. The precise colour reflected not only the amount of additives but also accidental impurities, temperature, the state of oxidation and the rate of cooling. In the most common process the molten glass mixture was extracted from the crucible with a pipe, blown up, then flattened into sheets. These sheets then found their way to the construction site, where the work of the glazier began.

The glazier began by cutting the sheets of glass according to the design drawn on the whitewashed table (see earlier) using a red-hot iron and water, and then shaped using a grozing iron. When the pieces were cut to the correct shapes the painting could begin. Hands, faces, and all other details were painted with a dark grey pigment onto the inner surface of the glass using badger, cat or pig bristle brushes, with each type of bristle giving a different effect. The pigment was made of copper or iron oxide, powdered glass, wine or urine and gum arabic. In addition to the main lines, a wash of paint – or a number of washes – was added for modelling, to give a three-dimensional effect. Sometimes details were then scratched out of these washes.

Each piece was then fired in the kiln to bind the paint. Very occasionally the glass was painted on the exterior surface for artistic effect – as, for example, at Waterperry or Beckley, both in Oxfordshire – although this 'back-painting' ran the risk of being quickly eroded by the weather if the window was in an exposed position. With the pieces painted and fired the window was then assembled on the table using lead cames (with an H-shaped cross section) to fit the composition together. Working from a corner, the lead held the glass in place under compression using 'closing nails' (spelt *clozyngnaill* in 1351!), the

lead pieces being soldered together to form the panel. Finally the panels were installed in the window opening by securing them to vertical stanchions or horizontal saddle bars with wire, which provided much-needed rigidity. In 12th- and 13th-century windows iron frames were used, often in strong geometric shapes such as circles, squares and quatrefoils that would also help the organization of the narrative.

Above: *The essentials of stained glass: pieces of glass coloured throughout their thickness, are cut to shape, painted, fired, and then held together by lead cames.* Below, far left and left: *Close examination of different panels (in this case at* **Canterbury***) show the same artist at work – these two panels by the 'Petronella Master' share the same furrowed brow, style of ears, hair locks, chin dimple, eye and nose lines.* Below, right and far right: *Two panels at* **Long Melford** *show yellow stain and back-painting being applied to the exterior side of the glass, and red glass being abraded to achieve the white crosses.*

was the narrative window, as seen in Canterbury's Bible windows of the late 12th century. The scenes of the story were typically divided using an iron armature pattern, and this style was used again in the 1220s in the Thomas Becket miracle windows. There is evidence that other narrative windows existed at this time, as isolated panels of the lives of Sts Alphege and Dunstan have survived. Lincoln Cathedral too probably had well-developed sequences, involving the life of Moses (and other Old Testament scenes), the lives of Sts Nicholas and John, the Childhood of Christ, and the life of the Virgin Mary. However, most of the glass that had survived there was rearranged in the 18th century.

While Gothic architecture is often thought of as a quest after lightness, many late 12th- and early 13th-century churches would actually have been very dark, since the glass is thick and the colours tend towards heavy reds and blues. Such glass dominates the space, and is often breathtaking. Perhaps it is the imperfections of the glass that play with the light, or perhaps it is the wonderfully fluid and expressive faces and drapery, but as one stands before the Becket miracle windows in the Trinity Chapel at Canterbury one senses that one is in the presence of a great secret that has since been lost. To many lovers of stained glass this early work has never been surpassed.

However, for all its beauty, by the second half of the 13th century it is clear that many architects, clergy and glaziers felt that this deep-coloured glass was making interiors too dark, and mysticism gave way to practicality. The alternative was to incorporate grisaille glass, which avoids nearly all colour, relying instead upon geometric, and later naturalistic foliage, designs painted onto the surface of clear – or sometimes pale green – glass. Grisaille had been favoured by the Cistercians since 1134, when St Bernard had forbidden the use of figurative panels and riotous colour. Examples of grisaille from the late 12th and early 13th centuries can be found around the country – for example, at Brabourne and Hastingleigh in Kent, and in the Stained Glass Museum, Ely. Later examples existed at Westminster Abbey (second half of the 13th century), and can still be seen at Salisbury Cathedral in Wiltshire (*c.* 1220–65). Although complete grisaille windows were common, the technique increasingly came to be found sandwiching coloured, figured panels, a compromise that allowed both colour and light, as well as being more economical than entirely coloured glazing. (Indeed, as windows

Grisaille from **St Mary, Hastingleigh**, Kent, c. 1200. The term grisaille derives from the French for 'grey'. Most of the window is made from white glass – or white with impurities that sometimes give it a green hue. This typical example of early grisaille has a geometric pattern with occasional small pieces of coloured glass. Such windows were more economical to produce, let in more light, and conformed to Cistercian demands for simple ornamentation that would not distract monks while praying.

grew larger with the progression from the Early English style to the Curvilinear and then the Perpendicular, the cost of the glazing became more and more of a consideration.) Fine examples of this sandwiching or 'band' style of grisaille can be seen at Merton College Chapel, Oxford, York Minster Chapter House (see pp. 26–7) and St Nicholas in Stanford-on-Avon. Colour in stained glass was always subject to fashion, as well as to the availability and affordability of the raw materials. In the second

decade of the 14th century a characteristic English stained glass style evolved showing a distinct scheme of red, green and yellow, occasional blue, and very carefully controlled areas of white glass. The figure drawing is often superb with genuine attempts at likeness or even portraiture (as, for example, at Madley – see pp. 56–7). Multiple narrative scenes, so popular in the 13th century, continue in the 14th century (as at Newark – see pp. 60–61), though generally in a reduced number of panels.

Left: In **York Minster** the five huge grisaille windows from *c.* 1250 in the north transept (known as the Five Sisters) contain over 100,000 pieces of glass. They are set into a series of complex geometric designs and incorporate coloured glass, but many of the individual pieces of glass carry a naturalistic design (now mostly faded) painted onto their surface.

Below: By the late 13th century, grisaille mixed with coloured panels had become popular, as seen here at **St Nicholas, Stanford-on-Avon**. The white grisaille is painted with oak leaves and acorns.

Donors and Heraldry

The practice of a church's benefactor having himself (or sometimes herself) immortalized in the windows – often with spouse and children – began in the 13th century, but became especially popular in the following century. The purpose, apart from reminding the congregation who the rich and powerful in the locality were, was to ingratiate the donors with God and to encourage future generations to pray for their souls in Purgatory. On some occasions donors to a church would even be offered papal indulgences (as happened in Tattershall in 1441).

Whatever the motivation, there was clearly no shortage of people keen to be depicted. At Merton College, Oxford, each of the depictions of the Twelve Apostles on either side of the nave is framed by a pair of kneeling figures. In fact each of these figures is the donor Henry Mamesfeld who thus appears no less than twenty-four times in the chapel! And donors were by no means limited to individuals and families. Guilds, too, were enthusiastic donors, as we can see from the bell founders' window in York (see p. 18), as were merchants, clergy, gentry and royalty (see

Canterbury and Malvern Priory). At the church of St Leonard, Middleton, the archers donated a window (see p. 34), while at the church of St Neot in Cornwall the glaziers themselves were the donors. The degree to which the donors dictated the position of 'their' windows in the building and the subject matter that was to be depicted is not entirely clear, but presumably they would have been able to ask for personal saints to be included.

That the donor was recognized was obviously very important, and the way in which donors might be identified changed over the ages. From the 15th century onwards we find real attempts at portraiture, but before then recognition was reliant either on inscriptions or on heraldry. The latter option was particularly popular in England from the early 14th century onwards, and superb examples of coats of arms, often set against grisaille, can be found at Selling, Norbury, Stanford-on-Avon, Wimpole and York Minster, among many other places. At Gloucester Cathedral the eighteen coats of arms that run along the base of the great east window may represent the leading knights who fought under King Edward III, either at Crécy in 1346 or elsewhere in France or

Above, left: *English 14th-century heraldic glass at its very best, at **St Mary of the Assumption, Froyle**, Hampshire, showing how the donors are related to the crown. At the top are the coats of arms of Edward the Confessor, then those of England and the heir. England appears again in the centre of the third row with those of Bohun and Warenne to left and right. In the bottom row are England, France ancient, Chastleton and Brotherton.* Above: *At **Long Melford** heraldry is continued on the clothing of the donors.*

Scotland. Heraldic glazing is also sometimes found in secular settings – very grand examples survive at Fawsley Hall (Northamptonshire) and Ockwells Manor (Berkshire). Heraldry also told the viewer of alliances between families and, where possible, relationships to the crown (as at Selling and Froyle).

There is also an important trend towards single figure compositions filling a single opening or 'light', as seen at Tewkesbury and Wells (see pp. 114 and 117). Some of these were further combined to create larger compositions – this is seen in the west window of York Minster, though it can also be found at the east windows of Gloucester and Exeter Cathedrals. At Gloucester the panels have been designed to fit into the rectilinear grid of

Cartoons were often reused, as can be seen in the east window at **Gloucester Cathedral**, *c.* 1357. By reversing the cartoon or part of it and separating the figures made from one cartoon with other designs the trick is less obvious.

tracery characteristic of the Perpendicular style. Within each of 56 of the 73 main openings is a figure of a saint, angel, martyr, king or ecclesiastic, set within the frame of a painted 'architectural' canopy. Such massive windows clearly posed a challenge to glaziers, who had to devise new techniques of economically covering such huge areas. A favourite device was to reuse the cartoons of the figure or the canopy, reversing the design from time to time to add variety. Such techniques had been used in the 13th century, but coupled with the greater use of white glass the glaziers attained a new efficiency (and economy). Gloucester's east window is also interesting for its substantial use of blue glass, by this point quite a rarity.

That the craft survived the devastating Black Death of the 1340s is clear from the large output in the second half of the 14th century. In fact those glaziers who survived became more highly valued, and while commissions did temporarily dry up, many survivors felt the need to thank God for the favour of being spared by donating to their church. Despite the war with France that was still being intermittently waged, church-building – and with it window-glazing – saw a considerable increase as society recovered. The Black Death also had an influence on iconography, and we tend to find more allusions to death and to the Last Judgment. At the church of All Saints, North Street, in York there is a graphic depiction of the Last Fifteen Days of the World, a rare and astonishing window from the early 15th century. In addition, the donors who helped build the churches and provide it with the glass were also increasingly keen to be depicted, sometimes with their families (see pp. 20 and 84). They often appear at the foot of the images they have given, exhorting us to pray for their souls in the afterlife (see p. 64).

Towards the end of the 14th century new colours were being introduced, such as deep purples and murrey-brown, and the portraiture becomes even more sophisticated in the hands of glaziers such as Thomas Glazier whose fine work can be seen at Winchester College (some of which is today in the Victoria and Albert Museum) and at New College, Oxford (see p. 65). Perhaps the most important technical development of the 14th century, however, was the introduction of the yellow stain technique. Up to that point all glass was coloured during the melt: the colour was more or less consistent throughout the sheet and decoration was confined to dark paint for features and shadow. In the 14th century, however, it was discovered that glass could also be *stained* yellow by painting a silver chemical onto its surface and then heating it (this process is the only time when stained glass is actu-

ally stained). The stain impregnated the surface of the glass and varied from pale yellow to almost orange, depending on the concentration used and how many times the process was repeated. The result was that an artist could create a single piece of glass with both white and yellow on it, giving rise to a far more delicate handling of colour. This technique was used sparingly to begin

Yellow stain is used in this 15th-century panel from **St Peter Mancroft, Norwich**, in three different ways: to produce the yellow of the Virgin's hair, the angels' wings and the thatch of the roof that the angels are working on; as a more orange tint when applied to the fireplace in the foreground; and on the blue glass of the Virgin's dress, to give a green pattern.

Daily Life in Stained Glass

Apart from the beauty of its colour and its interest and value to art historians, stained glass can also tell us a huge amount about everyday life throughout the medieval period. It was, after all, one of the most visible media of its time as far as ordinary, illiterate, people were concerned, and in showing people what they needed to know about their faith, these visual aids inadvertently say a lot about the society that created them.

So, alongside the important donors discussed earlier, we find other, humbler figures of artisans and tradespeople at work. Typically they are dressed in the clothing of the times (even in Biblical scenes), and an expert in the history of costume could probably trace fashions continuously over a 400-year period. At Long Melford the care with which the people are drawn reveals countless details about their dress and hairstyles, while the St Nicholas panels at Hillesden are rich in details of early 16th-century life (see pp. 23 and 107). Throughout the medieval period angelic musicians appear with a burgeoning collection of instruments – harps, organs, bells, flutes and shawms, timbrels, bagpipes, monochords, lutes and rebecs, to name just a few! – while in other Biblical scenes we find medieval doctors, fishermen and household wares. At the end of the medieval period, at King's College Chapel, Cambridge, alongside a whole range of hats, armour, shoes, boots and hairstyles, we find depictions of the latest architecture.

In the medieval period there was a much stronger connection with the land and with nature than there is today, and therefore it is no surprise to find depictions of flora, fauna and farming. Thirteenth-century depictions of wildlife are somewhat stylized with strange trees and bushes, often in even stranger colours; however, by the 15th century there is a large degree of realism – even if some of the animals in Noah's Ark at Malvern probably come from the glazier's imagination rather than from observation! Likewise some of the birds at Clothall (Hertfordshire), Yarnton, and in the Zouche Chapel at York Minster can be readily identified as robins and sparrows, though others are more challenging!

Left: *The bell founders at work in the window they gave to* **York Minster**. *Bells are to be found all over this window.* Below: *15th-century quarries at* **St Bartholomew, Yarnton***, depicting birds of the countryside. The quotations coming from the birds' beaks, such as 'who blayth this ayle...', suggest that these panes were probably made for an inn.*

with, but by the 15th century it had become widespread, especially as the cost of imported coloured glass escalated. In addition, in the 15th century the same stain was also applied to selected areas of blue glass to give two colours (blue and green) on the same panel (see p. 17), and even to abraded red glass, as seen at Long Melford (see p. 12).

Remains of 15th-century stained glass are widespread in England. There are particularly spectacular displays in the churches and the Minster in York, at Malvern Priory, and in churches in East Anglia and Cornwall. Glass of this period is recognizable from a number of characteristics: it is generally thinner; it appears in larger pieces; and its quality is more consistent than that of previous centuries. The colours are often less intense, yet the painting of faces and details is frequently of superb quality. In rare instances the attempts at realism are so keen that painting is carried out on both inner and outer surfaces of the glass, as with the figure of St Christopher at Beckley. White glass with plenty of yellow stain is used in abundance throughout the compositions. The architectural canopies and plinths framing figures and scenes that had grown vertically in the 14th century now expand laterally, sometimes with little figures lurking in the wings (as at York Minster). Perspective finds its way into the arrangement of the scenes, the architectural drawing of the surrounds, and particularly the chequered floors. The background 'seaweed' pattern that evolved in the 14th century (see, for example, Bolton Percy) becomes abundant in the 15th and is rarely found in colours other than red or blue.

By far the most common subjects in the 15th century were scenes from the Passion and figures of saints set beneath architectural canopies or on a plinth. As the century progressed cycles of the Virgin appeared (reflecting an increasing devotion to Mary), as well as more didactic subjects such as the Works of Mercy, and the Five Wounds of Christ, that would have been used in teaching the catechism.

In this century we also learn more about the glaziers themselves. For example, the 1405 contract between the glazier John Thornton of Coventry and York Minster's Dean and Chapter for the east window still exists, and it gives us a rare and valuable insight into the process of commissioning stained glass windows. Most interesting of all, it stipulates that John Thornton must personally carry out the painting, suggesting that the church

A 15th-century St Christopher carrying the Christ Child across a stream from Beckley. The glazier has painted the fish in the stream on the reverse side of the glass so as to give the impression of seeing them through the water.

authorities had had some bad experiences previously in relation to the quality of glazing work. Some thirty-five years later another contract – between the glazier John Prudde and the church authorities at the church of St Mary, Warwick, for the glazing of the Beauchamp Chapel – insists that only foreign glass is to be used. This seems to be a strange requirement considering that coloured glass had generally been imported anyway, but it may be referring to the English 'white' (clear) glass that was often off-white due to impurities in the sand and ash.

John Prudde was one of the last Englishmen to hold the post of Glazier to the King. From the middle of the 15th century glaziers from the Low Countries and Germany were increasingly settling in England, bringing the latest Continental styles in painting. The King in question – Edward IV, who had a Burgundian brother-in-law – was keen to be in the vanguard of all things Renaissance-inspired; he appears in the Royal window at Canterbury with his family, clearly portrayed by a Netherlandish hand. By the late 15th century so many foreign glaziers had found their way to Southwark (an important area for glazing) that a petition complaining about their number was presented by the London Glaziers' Company in 1474 and again in the 1520s.

The three youngest daughters of Edward IV – Anne, Catherine and Bridget – in the late 15th-century Royal window at **Canterbury**. The heads were renewed in the 18th century. A similar arrangement of a different royal family at the foot of a window can be seen at Malvern Priory in the north transept window (see p. 59).

Instruction and Education

One of the keenest debates in stained glass scholarship concerns the question of the intended audience for the windows and the role of stained glass as a teaching aid. Certainly in larger churches and cathedrals the congregation would not have had access to the entire building – only the clergy, for example, would have seen windows in the choir. Assuming that the congregation had access to the windows, though, what was their role in teaching? In the 19th century it was fashionable to see glass as a predecessor of the *Biblia Pauperum* – the highly illustrated Bible for the poor that became popular in the 15th century. In this view, the windows were actively used as visual aids in story-telling and teaching – some scholars even imagined the priest taking the congregation from window to window, almost as a modern guide would. Since the majority of the population would have been illiterate this is an appealing idea, and certainly the cartoon-like manner of display found in 12th- and 13th-century windows lends itself to story-telling with narratives such as the Childhood of Christ, the Passion, the Creation, and the lives of the Virgin Mary and the saints taking on a new vitality when presented in glass. However, glass is rarely so well organized within a church to be able to function as a form of Bible, and today such theories are seen as rather romantic.

Yet even if these windows were not used as direct teaching aids, all glass, as a fundamentally visible medium, has some didactic purpose. Depictions of

the Last Judgment, for example, were clearly designed to remind the faithful of the inevitable consequences of sin. Similarly the Crucifixion reminded the congregation of the essential truth of their religion. In later glass, however, we also find more concrete mnemonics of Christian duty, which do seem to function as catechisms. The Seven Sacraments of the Church – Baptism, Confirmation, Communion, Marriage, Penance, Holy Orders, Last Rites – can be seen at Tattershall (Lincolnshire), Buckland (Gloucestershire), Melbury Bubb (Somerset) and York Minster. Likewise the Works of Mercy – feeding the hungry, giving drink to the thirsty, clothing the naked, giving housing to the traveller, visiting prisoners, visiting the sick and burying the dead – that every Christian was supposed to perform can be seen at All Saints, North Street, in York (see p. 36), again at Tattershall and at Chinnor (Buckinghamshire) and Combs (Suffolk). The Penance Window in York Minster, meanwhile, shows penance being discussed – and applied with a whip!

Other aspects of the Church's liturgy find comfortable illustration in stained glass. The Apostles' Creed, for example, was thought in the Middle Ages to have been created by the Twelve Apostles as a joint venture and all twelve can sometimes be seen

Above: The Seven Deadly Sins often featured in the medieval Mystery Plays but are rarely found portrayed in stained glass. These two panels from **Newark** *feature Adultery and Avarice – they are tied to their sins by chains. Below: The famous 14th-century 'Gossip' window at* **Stanford-on-Avon***, where a pair of demons incite a pair of women to exchange gossip. Gossip may not be a Deadly Sin but it is denounced by St Paul in his Epistles.*

carrying a scroll bearing the sentence that they were deemed to have contributed – as at Fairford, Orchardleigh or Bolton Percy. The Virgin's *Magnificat* could be said to be 'expressed' in the north transept window at Malvern Priory where the Virgin Mary's role in the life of Christ is exalted across the six lights in the company of the four archangels. Likewise, remains of the Te Deum ('We praise thee O God') can be discerned at Beverley Minster (Humberside), at Morley (Derbyshire) and at York Minster. The Church's teaching in the moral sphere is, by contrast and perhaps surprisingly, somewhat rarely depicted in stained glass, and even when it is a pair of binoculars are helpful to see, for example, the Seven Deadly Sins at Newark and the problems of gossip at Stanford-on-Avon.

Saints, Angels and Devils

The most common subjects in church windows, by a long way, are saints and angels. Figures of saints appear as early as the 12th century (see Dalbury, p. 9), and their lives and deeds were supposed to be an inspiration to both parishioners and clergy. Over time they also came to act as intercessors between man and God. While some complete narrative windows of saints' lives have survived – for example, the adventures of St Anthony in the City of Dogs at Greystoke in Cumbria (see pp. 32–3), and scenes from the life of St Helen at Ashton under Lyne (p. 29) – more often saints appear as single figures. These are normally identifiable by their attributes or appearance. St Peter invariably has a key, Andrew a saltire cross; Bartholomew carries his flayed skin while Paul is bald; Barbara holds the tower in which she was imprisoned, Catherine the wheel on which she was tortured; Mary Magdalene has the ointment with which she washed Christ's feet, St Lucy her eyes that were gouged out; St Christopher, a saint popular with travellers and pilgrims, carries the Christ Child. St John can appear in a number of roles: as a young man at the Crucifixion, as an Apostle carrying a cup with a dragon (alluding to an attempt to poison him – see p. 57), as the Evangelist with an eagle, or seated on an island (Patmos) as supposed author of Revelation. Other saints had local origins, while others, such as Edward the Confessor, Edmund and Oswald, had a royal pedigree. Later generations, however, considered saints to be products of superstition, and for this reason such windows were a particular target of the iconoclasm following the Reformation.

Angels are essential attendants at the important events that define the evolving life of the Church, from the Annunciation to the Nativity where they attend the Virgin Mary, inform the shepherds in the fields, or illuminate the minds of the Wise Men. They appear again in some of the later medieval Crucifixion scenes, catching the blood of Christ or receiving the soul of the repentant thief, and are again present at the Resurrection informing the Holy Women of the momentous events. However, angels were far from equal, and every now and again the whole angelic hierarchy – from the Seraphim and Cherubim with six wings covered with eyes, down through Thrones, Dominations, Virtues, Powers and Principalities to the Archangels and Angels who appear on Earth to men and women – appears in stained glass, particularly in the 15th century. However, angels can also appear in more decorative settings, for example making music: in the east window at Warwick they even carry identifiable musical scores from which they sing, accompanied by their instrumental colleagues on the north side.

Devils and demons are, mercifully, less prominent although they play their part when required (causing accidents and illness in the 13th century, or encouraging evil deeds in the 16th, and always appearing at the Last Judgment to claim unrepentant souls). Wherever they appear, glaziers never cease to surprise us with the originality of their monsters. The most impressive devils of all can be found at Fairford, where they lurk over the heads of the figures on the north side nave clearstorey, who are appropriately named Enemies of the Church, some of whom carry swords and decapitated heads.

Left: *An angel sounding a trumpet of Last Judgment from the Lady Chapel in* **Wells Cathedral**.

Below: *Two of the demons above the Enemies of the Church at* **Fairford**.

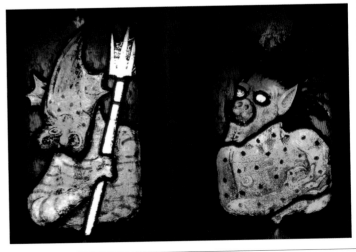

The change in tastes, design and execution that arrived in England after the 1470s arguably reached its high point at two very important sites: King's College Chapel, Cambridge and the church of St Mary, Fairford. In both cases the leading artists were from abroad, respectively Galyon Hone from the Low Countries and Barnard Flower possibly from Germany. Continuing the trend that had begun in the 14th century, large painterly 'canvases' are spread across the windows' lights with little regard for the stone tracery. Indeed, by this point glass painting is sometimes regarded as an offshoot of panel painting, and at Cambridge some of the later designs (carried out by Dirk Vellert) clearly rely on woodcuts, including some by Albrecht Dürer. One downside of this approach is that the leading around the figures conflicts with the regular matrix of rectangular quarries, making the excellence of the work difficult to appreciate from afar. However, the loss of legibility is to some extent made up for by the fantastic, Renaissance-inspired painting of people, beasts, angels and devils. At Hillesden in Buckinghamshire there are some marvellous characters amid the scenes drawn by English artists clearly inspired by the artists from abroad. In the chapel of The Vyne, a stately home near Basingstoke, Hampshire, the early 16th-century glass was apparently executed by glaziers from Calais. Continental glaziers were also very active at the royal establishments of Richmond Palace, the Savoy Chapel, Windsor, Eltham and Greenwich Palaces and the Henry VII chapel at Westminster Abbey, but apart from Windsor almost all of this glass is now lost. (A few pieces remained at Westminster until the Second World War.)

The era of stained glass, along with church-building generally, came to an abrupt end in the 1530s. Increasing differences with Pope Clement VII led Henry VIII to break away from the Catholic communion, disband the monasteries, and establish the Church of England. The resulting destruction was considerable, and large amounts of glass disappeared as buildings were dismantled or abandoned. Much of that which did survive suffered a similar fate one hundred years later during the English Civil War (1642–9) at the hands of 'Parliamentary Visitors' such as William Dowsing, who kept a diary of his vandalism as he swept through East Anglia. Where glass survived it was often due to the intervention of men such as Lord Fairfax, who secured the surrender of the city of York on the grounds that his men would not ravage

Bizarre faces and expressions in Renaissance-inspired glass at **All Saints, Hillesden**, early 16th century. In this scene, following a warning from St Nicholas, thieves return the treasure they have stolen to avoid eternal damnation.

the city's churches. Elsewhere it was up to villagers to protect their treasures by hiding them, some to be discovered only much, much later. At the church of Selling in Kent the magnificent 14th-century east window (see p. 113) was found in the 19th century hidden within the church's walls; in other cases glass survived in crypts or local manor houses, or else has since been excavated from nearby sites.

The vandalism did not end there, however. Tastes had moved on, and by the time of the Restoration of Charles II there was little appetite for stained glass – the churches of Wren and Hawksmoor were generally glazed with white glass, and the 18th century saw many more losses as medieval windows were replaced with more up-to-date glass. Much of the medieval glass at Salisbury was ignominiously abandoned in the town rubbish dump and the lead recycled as part of James Wyatt's 1788–91 'restoration' of the cathedral. Some of the glass found its way onto the antiquities market, where it ended up in the hands of a few enlightened souls who were beginning to take an interest in England's medieval heritage. Other panels were salvaged and later returned to the cathedral or placed in parish churches. (Stained glass is a very portable medium, and panels often end up in other churches.) Happily, the interest of a few antiquarians had, by the mid-19th century, grown into a much broader interest in the medieval arts known today as the Gothic Revival. Stained glass studios rediscovered some of the lost techniques, giving an impetus both to newly established Victorian glass firms such as Hardman, Warrington and Clayton & Bell, but particularly to the Arts and Crafts style of windows exemplified by Morris & Co. This also enabled ancient damaged windows to be repaired and 'completed' using glass that bore at least some resemblance to the original medieval material – indeed, in some cases scholars have been at a loss to say which is old and which is new.

Today stained glass is better understood and appreciated than ever before, but with the growing scholarship has come the realization that only a fraction of the original medieval glass in England has survived – some estimates put the figure as low as ten per cent. And even today, when society feels less inclined to attack stained glass windows directly, they remain vulnerable to pollution. Glass is inherently fragile and for windows to survive intact for even a century requires regular attention, cleaning and maintenance. Some of the large cathedrals have sophisticated workshops that can look after and conserve the glass, but the others, along with smaller churches and chapels, are often reliant on the expertise and funding of local communities and national heritage organizations.

This conservation, in turn, reflects the growing importance given to stained glass within the broader study of medieval arts and society. Since few original documents relating to individual stained glass windows have survived, scholarship has often had to rely upon other methods for dating the glass, deducing the sequence of glazing schemes from building dates, comparisons of styles with other locations or media, or by identifying the donors associated with the installations. Chief among the various organizations working to preserve this heritage is the Corpus Vitrearum Medii Aevi, an international stained glass research project that for the past fifty or so years has catalogued the surviving medieval stained glass, county by county. The details of some of their catalogues and associated works can be found at the back of this book. With such projects, and hopefully through publications such as this one, medieval stained glass will continue to bring joy and enlightenment for at least another 900 years.

Conservation

Even glass that has survived war, iconoclasm, vandalism and dubious restoration will not last long without regular attention. Leading becomes lose, windows leak and distort, and the surface is weakened and battered by both pollution and the elements. Bad firing and abrasion can result in the erosion of painted details such as faces and drapery, and a number of chemical reactions continuously take place between air, water and the glass that lead to the formation of a kind of patina (especially in glass containing potassium, which is susceptible to acidic rain). This patina eventually renders the glass opaque, and if left untreated can flake off, making the glass thinner and even creating holes right through it.

Thus it is not uncommon to find 14th- and 15th-century repairs to 13th-century windows. In the 16th and 17th centuries, however, there was little conservation, and in the 18th century attempts were often crude – see, for example, the 18th-century heads in 14th- and 15th-century windows at York Minster, where either the original flesh-coloured glass

*Modern glue has been used to reassemble the face of Elizabeth Dinham at **Long Melford** without ugly lead lines.*

iconography with creating an arrangement that sits comfortably with its neighbours. Restoration of an original window is always the preferred option, but this is a time-consuming and therefore expensive undertaking. Worse, for many years there was no real policy guiding restoration even though the practice has been going on from the day the windows were created. However, over the past forty or so years a policy and practice has gradually evolved where there is at last some measure of international agreement: for example, chemicals are no longer used in the cleaning and preservation of the glass.

A modern restoration, then, begins by photographing the window and tracing the lead patterns precisely, as well as recording any other observations concerning both the condition of the

Left: Tough isothermal glazing at **Canterbury** *protects the restored window. Below: Much repair work in the studio takes place on a light table, although the final panels will be held up to natural light to ensure that any replacement glass fits in harmoniously with the original old pieces.*

window as a whole and the individual pieces of glass. The window is then dismantled and each piece of glass is laboriously cleaned with a soft wad and water, the more resilient pieces of patina being abraded away with a delicate tool, sometimes in conjunction with a microscope. Loose paint is resealed with resin but no new painting is carried out on old glass. Sometimes missing lettering is painted onto a second piece of new glass placed behind the old piece. The pieces are then reassembled in a new network of lead, and to ensure their survival in the future attempts are made to protect the newly restored window from the elements. The ideal solution is to set the window into a new frame a few centimetres inside its original position, and to fill the slots in the masonry with an isothermal glazing system. This is essentially a screen made from pieces of tough transparent material with a similar leading pattern to the original panels. This keeps out rain, wind, hail, stones and errant cricket balls while allowing a flow of air over the outer surface of the stained glass.

had been of inferior quality or else the faces were knocked out to appease the Puritan iconoclasts. In the 19th century an inspired amateur approach to restoration often resulted in a kind of creative reconstruction of the window, filling in missing pieces either with other medieval glass or with modern pieces. However, from the middle of that century Charles Winston's researches into how medieval glass was made allowed decent, authentic pot-metal glass to became available again. Messrs Powell of Whitefriars in London and Chance Brothers in Birmingham started manufacturing glass in accordance with Winston's discoveries, and coupled with research into medieval design principles gave birth both to more accurate restoration as well as to a new industry of Victorian stained glass.

Conservators today face many dilemmas. For example, where panels are missing should they be replaced with new panels in a medieval design, new panels using modern designs, filled with white glass, or replaced with medieval panels from another location? They must balance recreating the original

The North

WHILE SURVIVALS of medieval glass in the north of England have been patchy, the region is also home to the single most important city for stained glass, York. The highlight there is the Minster, which has over one hundred windows with glass from the 12th to 16th centuries, but the city has many other churches with substantial remains of medieval glass. Of these Holy Trinity, Goodramgate, has some of the most beautifully detailed 15th-century glass (see pp. 38–9), while All Saints, North Street, has, among other unusual windows, an extraordinary and rare Last Fifteen Days of the World (pp. 36–7). Other places in the city include fine panels at St Michael, Spurriergate, St Denys, Walmgate, St Martin le Grand and All Saints, Pavement.

The influence of the York 'school' of glass painters can be found in several other places in the North (as well as in other parts of the country), even on the west coast – for example, at St Andrew, Cartmel Fell, Cumbria. Elsewhere in Cumbria we find fascinating 14th-century Last Judgment figures at Carlisle Cathedral, and one of the highlights of 16th-century glass anywhere in the country at Greystoke, where there survives a unique depiction of the supposed adventures of St Matthew and St Andrew in the City of Dogs. Further south, at Ashton under Lyne, there are some unusual panels with scenes from the life of St Helen as well as some fine depictions of English kings. Nor are the seventeen English archer-donors at nearby Middleton to be missed.

Other important locations include Acaster Malbis, Beverley Minster, Bolton Percy, Durham Cathedral, Easby, Lanchester and Thornhill, all of which have at least some fine medieval pieces (including, at St Agatha, Easby, significant remains from the 12th century).

The Chapter House, York Minster, building and glass late 13th century.

Acaster Malbis (North Yorkshire)

Holy Trinity / Mid-14th century

Right: These panels in the east window were recently
repaired and rearranged by the York Glaziers' Trust,
helping make sense of the previously mixed-up figures.
From left to right are St Andrew, a female saint, a male
saint (maybe St Paul, but with a later female head),
St James with shells on his clothing, St Bartholomew
carrying his flayed skin (as at Grappenhall – see
p. 32), and two further saints carrying books.
Below: The figure of Christ blessing is in a superb
state of preservation.

Ashton under Lyne

(Greater Manchester)

St Michael and All Angels / Late 15th century

Above: The windows at Ashton under Lyne were given by Sir Thomas Ashton and contain a rare depiction of twenty scenes from the life of St Helen. These figures are doctors attending the saint's conversion to Christianity. The characterization and the bulbous noses strongly suggest the work of glaziers from York.

29

Bolton Percy (North Yorkshire)

All Saints / 15th century

Opposite: The fine east window has survived more or less intact though with much restoration. The main figures, left to right, are St Peter, St Anne teaching the Virgin to read, the Virgin and Child, St Elizabeth and St John. Beneath are three archbishops and two bishops: from left to right, Paulinus, Chad, Wilfrid, John of Beverley and William. They are reminiscent of figures in York Minster. Along the bottom are the coats of arms of the families Scrope, Bowitt, Kempe, Booth and Neville. In the tracery lights amid angels and archangels the female saints include Agnes, Dorothy, Barbara, Mary Magdalene, Veronica.
Left: St Mary Magdalene from the tracery lights.

Carlisle (Cumbria)

Carlisle Cathedral / Second half 14th century

Below: Scenes from the Last Judgment fill all of the tracery lights in the magnificent east window at Carlisle Cathedral. Here, figures rise from their graves as angels sound trumpets.

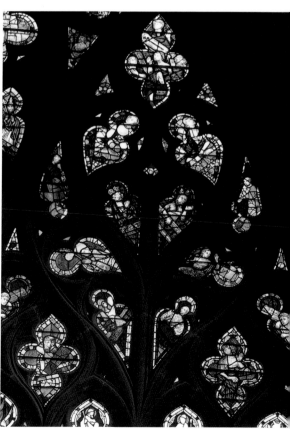

Grappenhall (Cheshire)

St Wilfrid / Mid-14th century

Above: A detail from the east window at Grappenhall, which contains a number of 14th-century figures in good condition. St Bartholomew, in a medieval attempt at realism, drapes his flayed skin over his arm like a coat!

Greystoke (Cumbria)

St Andrew / c. 1520

Right and opposite: Three of the nine panels recomposed in 1898 in the east window of Greystoke parish church. The text associated with the panels suggests they refer to the apocryphal legend of St Matthew and St Andrew in the City of Dogs and in the City of Wronden, inhabited, it was believed, by cannibals. How these panels relate to the story told in the text above them is not immediately clear, however. *Right, above:* Christ beckons a group in a boat, one of whom is fishing. *Right:* Christ, flanked by St Peter and St Andrew. *Opposite:* A composite panel of a king (probably St Oswald of Northumbria), St Andrew at the gate of a castle, a figure in prison and a person being baptized. The window highlights the difficulties faced by restorers trying to make sense of seemingly unrelated scenes.

Middleton (Greater Manchester)

St Leonard / 1505

Opposite: This window contains fragments at the top and a collection of donor figures below, which includes Sir Richard Assheton, his wife, children and chaplain Henry Tayler. However, the highlight is the depiction of the donor archers of Middleton – seventeen of them, each named and carrying his bow and arrows. They were formerly thought to have fought at the battle of Flodden Field (1513) but the date in the window of 1505 suggests they were Sir Edward Stanley's own troop of archers.

York (North Yorkshire)

All Saints, Pavement / *c.* 1370

Below, left and right: The glass at All Saints, Pavement, began life in the nearby, and now redundant, church of St Saviour. Although somewhat fractured and darkened, we still see clearly in eleven of the panels scenes from the Passion cycle up to the Ascension; it is work by the York school. In these two scenes we see the Resurrection and the doubting Thomas putting his hand into Christ's wound.

York (North Yorkshire)

All Saints, North Street / Early 15th century

The subject matter of this remarkable window is very rare (the only other stained glass depiction is in the 15th-century north rose window in Angers). Based on the poem 'The Prykke of Conscience', it is a depiction of the Last Fifteen Days of the World. *Opposite:* The sequence begins at the bottom, and runs left to right: (Day 1) the sea rises submerging the trees; (Day 2) it falls again; (Day 3) it returns to its former level; (Day 4) fish and sea monsters cry out from the deep; (Day 5) the sea catches fire; (Day 6) the trees catch fire; (Day 7) earthquakes; (Day 8) rocks and stones disappear into the earth; (Day 9) people try to escape by hiding in holes; (Day 10) only the earth and sky can be seen; (Day 11) people emerge from their holes to pray; (Day 12) the bones of the dead emerge from their coffins; (Day 13) the stars fall from heaven; (Day 14) death visits everyone; (Day 15) the all-consuming fire of the end. The details on this page show Day 14 (*above left*) and Day 5 (*above right*). It is thought to have been painted by the workshop of John Thornton, which also worked on the great east window at York Minster. *Left:* A panel from another cycle at the church showing the Seven Works of Mercy (see p. 21) – this one shows Visiting the Prisoners. The same wealthy bearded figure with hat, fine cloak and ermine appears in each scene; here he visits the unfortunate prisoners locked in the stocks. He holds a pouch while a guard keeps watch with a stick.

York (North Yorkshire)

Holy Trinity, Goodramgate / 15th century

Opposite: This remarkable east window contains very
fine glass of the York school. The main figures are
(left to right) St George, John the Baptist, the Trinity
(God the Father holds the Crucified Son and the dove
represents the Holy Spirit), St John and St Christopher.
Below them are St Mary Cleophas with her family
(including Jude, Simon, James the Less and Joseph
Justus); then St Anne, Joachim and the Virgin;
another depiction of the Trinity; Salome and Zebedee
with St John the Baptist; and St Ursula protecting
some of the thousand virgins (and a pope and a
king). At the top are coats of arms including those
of Canterbury (second from left) and John Kemp,
Archbishop of York 1425–62 (centre). *Right:* A detail
of the Trinity, represented as three figures at the
Coronation of the Virgin Mary (the head of the latter
has been replaced with that of a donor). *Below:*
A number of beautiful reset 15th-century fragments,
including a fine eagle perched on a young saint's arm.

York (North Yorkshire)

St Denys, Walmgate / c. 1350 and 15th century

Left: This church has glass of the 13th, 14th, 15th and 16th centuries in a number of windows. In this panel from a mid-14th-century window in the north aisle, the donor, Robert of Skelton (a chamberlain and bailiff in York) gives a window. The background is made up of a field of quarries depicting butterflies. *Above:* In a 15th-century panel amid fragments on the south side of the church, a pope receives evil counsel from a woman and a demon.

York (North Yorkshire)

St Michael, Spurriergate / 15th century

A number of windows in this church have survived with their glass reasonably intact. *Opposite, left:* The 'Woman Clothed with the Sun and with the Moon Under Her Feet' from the Book of Revelation. She carries the 'Man-Child' and is set in a mandorla frame studded with 'jewels'. Beneath are Lucifer and his fallen angels. *Opposite, right:* A rare depiction of the angelic hierarchy, showing eight of the nine members: top to bottom, left to right they are: Seraphim, Cherubim, Thrones, Virtues, Principalities, Powers, Dominions and Angels – the Archangels are absent.

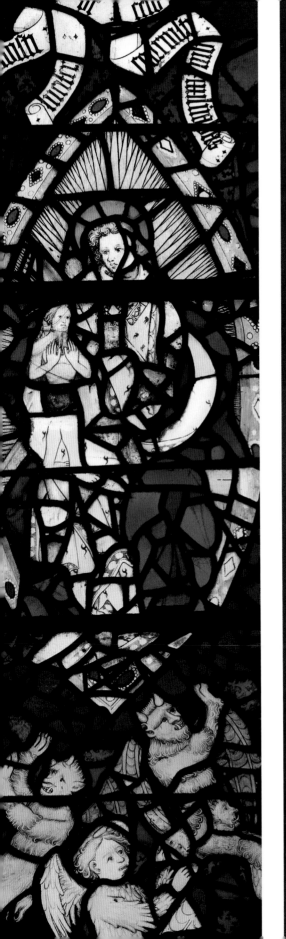

York (North Yorkshire)

York Minster

The stained glass at York Minster is world-famous, and deservedly so. It spans all periods from the 12th to 20th centuries but is particularly rich in glass from the 14th and 15th centuries. In one of the Chapter House windows and high in the nave are a number of reset panels probably from the old 12th-century choir built by Archbishop Roger. The Chapter House also contains a splendid display of band-style grisaille and coloured panels of the late 13th century. In the main body of the Minster the famous Five Sisters window (see p. 14) also dates from the 13th century, while the great west window of the 14th century by Master Robert is generally in superb condition. Other 14th-century glass can be seen high in the choir clearstorey, in the nave and in the choir aisles. The glorious 15th-century east window with hundreds of panels painted by John Thornton of Coventry (161 in the main lights, 117 in the traceries) has been undergoing restoration in recent years; Thornton's other great work is the St William window, in the north-east transept. The Minster also houses glass from a number of other churches in the city and even some from further afield, such as a Tree of Jesse from New College Chapel Oxford.

Opposite, above: Part of a series of thirty panels depicting the Te Deum, from *c.* 1420, transferred from the church of St Martin-le-Grand, Coney Street, York, and now in the south transept. Here we see God the Creator with medieval dividers and the orb of authority. Birds, animals and two humans in a boat surround Him. *Opposite, below:* Two of the 12th-century panels from the earlier building (now reset high in the nave clearstorey) showing souls being tormented at the Last Judgment, some in a boiling pot, others in the Mouth of Hell.

Left: The prophet Isaiah in magnificent mid-15th-century glass in the south choir. The canopy above Isaiah's head contains little angels, saints, lions and birds, a defining feature of York school glass. *Above:* The donors of the St William window, members of the de Ros family. This window, from *c.* 1421, is by John Thornton of Coventry.

Overleaf, left: The rose window in the south transept. The design and much of the stonework dates from the mid-13th century; the glass is 16th century. The white and red roses celebrate the union of the Houses of York and Lancaster in 1486. At the centre is a sunflower from the 18th century by William Peckitt. Although much affected by the fire in 1988, careful preservation has ensured that much of the original glass has been retained. *Overleaf, right:* Five of the eight lancets of the great west window, the gift of Archbishop William Melton in the mid-14th century, glazed by Master Robert and still in fine condition after over 600 years. At the bottom are Archbishops of York, Melton's predecessors (many of the faces are 18th-century replacements). In the centre are the Twelve Apostles, some in pairs to fill the eight lancets: here, left to right, are two pairs, then St John carrying an eagle, St Peter with a church and St Paul with a sword. In the top row we see the Annunciation (two panels), the Nativity (two panels) and the Resurrection.

43

The Midlands

THE MIDLANDS is home to what is probably the oldest stained-glass panel in England, the haunting depiction of St Michael at Dalbury, Derbyshire, which dates (at the latest) to the early 12th century. Glass of the following century is particularly well represented at Lincoln Cathedral, including a marvellous rose window, and at Ashbourne in Derbyshire, but the region is especially strong in glass from the 14th century, notably at Merevale, Madley, Eaton Bishop, Lowick, Norbury, Newark, Woodborough and, above all, at Stanford-on-Avon in Northamptonshire.

Coventry was undoubtedly an important centre for glassmakers in medieval times – indeed, John Thornton of Coventry made the magnificent glass in York Minster's east window between 1405 and 1408. Coventry Cathedral itself was lost during the Second World War, but there remain some fine 15th-century portrayals of English kings at St Mary's Guildhall in the city (see pp. 6–7). Other highlights of 15th-century glass include Malvern Priory, which boasts a rare depiction of William the Conqueror, and the Beauchamp Chapel at St Mary, Warwick, which has another characteristically English figure, Thomas Becket. The angelic choir and musicians here are superb with their accurate depictions of musical scores and instruments.

The single most important city in the south of the Midlands is Oxford where much of the glass survived the post-Reformation vandalism. Of the university colleges, Christ Church has some fine 14th-century panels and unusual tracery lights, while Merton had a particularly eager donor in the form of Henry Mamesfeld; other colleges with good collections include New College and All Souls.

The east end of the Beauchamp Chapel, St Mary, Warwick, with glass by John Prudde of Westminster, 1440–62.

Ashbourne (Derbyshire)
St Oswald / 13th century

Above: One of the five 13th-century panels in the church almost certainly contemporary with its building, showing the Adoration of the Magi. Although some of the painted features have been lost, the glass retains the colourfulness and intimacy characteristic of the finest 13th-century work.

Beckley (Oxfordshire)
Assumption of the Blessed Virgin Mary / 14th century

Right: This church has some fine 14th-century panels depicting the Glorification of the Virgin Mary. Here she is giving her girdle to St Thomas at the time of her Assumption. This strange scene comes from apocryphal sources that were popular around the year 1300, after Westminster Abbey had acquired a relic that included a part of the girdle.

Checkley (Staffordshire)
St Mary and All Saints / Early 14th century

Opposite: This early 14th-century east window is made up of alternating coloured panels with very beautiful patterned grisaille. In the top row of coloured panels we see (left to right) St Chad, a young St John, St Thomas Becket, St Thomas and a bishop (maybe St Nicholas). The lower row features the stoning of St Stephen, Abraham about to sacrifice Isaac, the Crucifixion, St Margaret with the dragon and the murder of Thomas Becket.

Coventry (West Midlands)
St Mary's Guildhall / 1450s
Above and left: St Mary's Guildhall at Coventry was
built in the early 1340s, some thirty years before the
old cathedral. Royalty was recorded to have stayed
there on certain occasions, and the row of nine kings
in the huge stained glass window celebrates kingship
in all its glory – Kings Arthur and Constantine feature
– but particularly the Lancastrian dynasty. At the
centre is Henry VI from whom the Guildhall obtained
a charter. The glass has been said to be by John
Thornton of Coventry (famous for the great east
window in York Minster): it is certainly his style.

Eaton Bishop (Herefordshire)
St Michael and All Angels / Early 14th century
Right: The east window of Eaton Bishop's parish
church is one of the glories of English 14th-century
glass. On the far left is the Virgin and Child, then
St Michael, a bishop beneath the Crucifixion, the
archangel Gabriel and a fragmentary panel. In the
bottom row the donor Adam de Muirimouth appears
twice below the archangels, while overhead are some
superb canopies showing gothic flying buttresses –
with birds in their midst. *Opposite:* Details of St
Michael weighing a human soul (*above*), and one
of the remarkable canopies (*below*).

51

Hereford (Herefordshire)

Hereford Cathedral / c. 1300

Left: An unusual depiction of Christ between the symbols of the Evangelists set against darkened grisaille. Traditionally this symbolizes Christ as the Word of God as promulgated by the Gospels: the Lion is the symbol of St Mark, the Bull of St Luke, the Eagle of St John and the Angel of St Matthew. The face of Christ is particularly individualized.

Kidlington (Oxfordshire)

St Mary / 15th century

Below: The east window of this church is an assembly of various pieces of glass that survived the centuries. In this panel of the Trinity, God the Father holds the crucified Son and the Holy Spirit appears as a dove between them. God is in fact made up from two different panels and the crucified Christ is a modern panel, yet the face of God gives the scene great power.

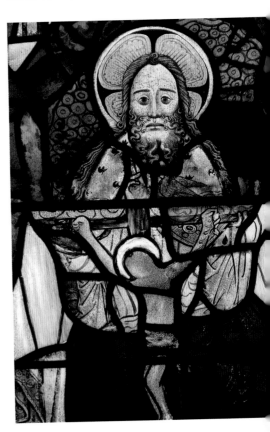

Kingerby (Lincolnshire)

St Peter / 14th century

Above and right: In such a tiny church in Lincolnshire it is a joy to come across such an excellent 14th-century window, showing St Catherine with her wheel and St Cecilia playing the organ (the faces are modern). These female saints were especially appropriate since at the time the window was made the church supported the convent at Elsham.

Lincoln (Lincolnshire)

Lincoln Cathedral

By the end of the 13th century Lincoln Cathedral must have had an impressive collection of stained glass, with two spectacular rose windows. However, the ideological vandalism of the 16th and 17th centuries left the cathedral's glass in a sorry state, and during the second half of the 18th century some 'tidying up' was carried out which in many respects only compounded the jumble. The lancets beneath the rose windows were consolidated, while other surviving panels and fragments were assembled into the east windows of the choir aisles, as well as being used to fill in gaps in the north rose window. The remains indicate, however, that there must originally have been an extensive programme of Old and New Testament subjects.

Of the rose windows, the north – referred to in the 13th-century 'Metrical Life of St Hugh' as the 'Dean's Eye' – retains much of its original glass. The south – known as the 'Bishop's Eye' – would probably have matched the north originally, but was rebuilt in the 14th century and contains only fragments of glass of that period.

Left: St Barnabus reset in grisaille in the east window of the south aisle, *c.* 1230. *Below:* Moses leads the Children of Israel across the Red Sea while the Pharaoh and his chariots perish in the sea, also in the east window of the south aisle, *c.* 1230.

Opposite: The magnificent north rose window dates from the 1220s and retains about seventy per cent of its original glass. This, and its size, makes it one of the most significant roses in Europe, and highly reminiscent of the contemporary window at Lausanne. The original theme of the glass was the Last Judgment but over the centuries panels from other parts of the cathedral have found their way into the composition. The outer circle still contains some original panels with angels holding instruments of the Passion and the Elect being led off to Paradise, while the bishops and the Adam and Eve panel are interpolations. Cleaning of the glass and reconstruction of the stonework, begun in the 1980s, was completed in 2006.

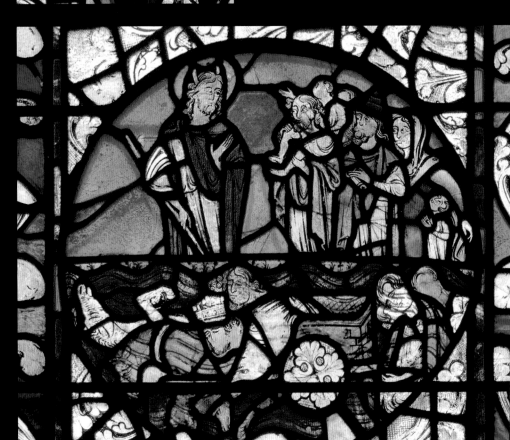

Madley (Herefordshire)

Nativity of the Blessed Virgin Mary / 13th and 14th centuries

Although Madley church was completed in 1320 it contains glass from a number of different periods, including, strangely, the 13th century. The best of this early glass is to be found in the east window, and includes the two panels *opposite, above*. The left-hand panel shows the Adoration of the Magi, while the right-hand panel shows St John with Aristodemus – the latter did not believe in the saint's powers and tested him with a poison that had already killed two men (one lies dead on the ground). John survived and Aristodemus was converted. The east window also contains 14th-century glass, some of which suggests the presence at some point of a particularly beautiful Tree of Jesse dating to around 1340–50: *left*, we see the Prophet Ezekiel; *below*, we see the king Josiah. *Opposite, below:* Two fragmentary figures of bishops in the east window, also from the 14th century.

Malvern (Worcestershire)

Malvern Priory

Malvern Priory contains one of the finest collections of medieval glass in the country. The glazing took some time, and we can detect the hands of a number of glass painters, including those of the 15th-century York school of glaziers, as well as Richard Twygge and Thomas Wodshawe. On the south side of the church is a collection of Old Testament panels with some beautiful drawing, deeply coloured glass and fascinating details – a good example would be the Adam and Eve panel. The church also has a rare example of a 'Founder's window' high up in the chancel, where the Hierarchy of the Angels can also be seen; the chancel also boasts an equally rare portrayal of William the Conqueror.

At first sight much of the glass in the huge east window (see p. 1) seems to be somewhat fragmentary, but some time spent studying it reveals many gems and complete panels including donors, many scenes from a Passion sequence, and a near-complete series of apostles in the tracery lights. The final window to be installed in the church was the early 16th-century transept window given by the king.

Opposite: The Founder's window with St Werstan's Vision, 15th century. St Werstan prays on a hillside where four angels mark out on the ground (complete with a primrose and a harebell) where St Werstan is to build a chapel – the future Malvern Priory.

Above: The rebuke of Adam and Eve, 15th century. This scene forms part of the fine Old Testament series in the south chapel.

Right: The astonishing Magnificat window, dedicated to the Virgin Mary. The main scenes show events from Christ's life where his mother was also present, from the Annunciation to the Ascension. The Coronation of the Virgin, spanning three lancets, off-centre, is marked out with a golden ring and her blue vesica. The figures at the foot include (right to left) Henry VII, his wife, Prince Arthur, Sir Reginald Bray, Sir John Savage and Sir Thomas Lovell.

Merevale (Warwickshire)

Our Lady / Mid-14th century

Left: The fine glass at Merevale is probably by
the same West Midlands workshop that did the
Annunciation at Hazdor (now in the Stained Glass
Museum, Ely – see p. 81) and some of the figures in
the Latin Chapel in Christ Church, Oxford (see p. 63).
The detail here shows Solomon from a Tree of Jesse.

Newark (Nottinghamshire)

St Mary Magdalene / 14th and 15th centuries

Right: The highlight at Newark is the east window of
the south chapel where in the 1950s Joan Howson
set 14th-century panels between 15th-century scenes
or assemblages of fragments. The 14th-century
panels are, unusually for a parish church, all in colour
with little grisaille and include the Creation, Adam
and Eve being expelled from Eden, the Magi and
Christ in the Temple, the Last Supper, Gethsemene
and Last Judgment figures. Of the 15th-century
panels, in the leftmost lancet are various figures
including a pope, a king, a saint, St Etheldreda and a
Trinity panel; in the second lancet are scenes from the
Childhood of Christ and a lute player. The fifth lancet
includes a rare portrayal of Joseph being attacked by
the Virgin's suitors (see the detail *below*), while the
sixth contains fragments that include an identifiable
St Catherine and a Candlemas procession.

Norbury (Derbyshire)

St Mary and St Barlok / 15th century

Above: The chancel of this church has a magnificent display of medieval glass. The east window contains an assembly of panels from around the church including St Peter carrying the book of the Word and his traditional emblem of the keys, while above his head is his supposed contribution to the Apostles' Creed: 'Credo in unum deum; pater omnipotentem; creator celi et terra' – I believe in one God, Father Almighty, Maker of Heaven and Earth. On the north and south sides of the chancel are some fine 14th-century panels with coats of arms set against grisaille.

Oxford (Oxfordshire)

University of Oxford College Chapels

A number of the Oxford college chapels are particularly rich in medieval stained glass, notably Merton (late 13th, 14th and 15th centuries), Christ Church (mid-14th century), New College (late 14th century) and All Souls (15th century). Whereas Merton is much focused on its donor, Henry Mamesfeld, Christ Church has some classical 14th-century figures in the Latin Chapel and some bizarre stained glass grotesques in the Lucy Chapel; New College again features its founder together with a galaxy of Old and New Testament figures and saints by Thomas Glazier, while a John Glazier (possibly Thomas's son) created a similar suite at All Souls College that focused on English royalty as well as on the Old and New Testaments.

All Souls College Chapel
Left: St John portrayed as a young man, holding the poisoned chalice (symbolized by a small dragon), c. 1447. Most of the glass in the antechapel, where the Twelve Apostles are matched by twelve female saints, is by John Glazier and dates from 1440–47.
Below: St Jerome with the Bible and the lion, set against some fine painted quarries, on the north side of the great west window at All Souls.

Christ Church College Chapel

Left: St Cuthbert carrying St Oswald's head, *c.* 1330, from the Lucy Chapel. This unusual scene stems from the fact that when St Cuthbert's relics were translated from Lindisfarne, St Oswald's head was put into the coffin! *Below:* The murder of Thomas Becket by the four knights, *c.* 1330, again from the Lucy Chapel. It is not dissimilar to the scene in the east window at Checkley (see p. 49). *Right:* St Catherine carries the wheel on which she was tortured, *c.* 1360, from the Latin Chapel. There is delicate use of yellow stain, as well as attempts at perspective in the canopies over the saint's head.

Merton College Chapel

Left: The 14th-century rose atop the east window, with glass containing the coats of arms of England, the Prince of Wales and Clare.
Below: Henry Mamesfeld appears twice here as the donor framing St Peter. The late 13th-century coloured panels are set against grisaille in a band that runs through all of the windows on the north and south sides of the chapel; Mamesfeld thus appears some 24 times.

New College Chapel

Opposite: At first sight these figures, from 1380–86, seem to be three female saints, but the trio is actually a transformed Crucifixion with Mary on the left and John on the right carrying a book. The bottom of the cross is just visible below the central female figure that seems to have replaced the Crucifixion. There are four such similar scenes in the chapel, with figures set within formidable canopies and substantial plinths, below the Twelve Apostles in the east windows of the antechapel by Thomas Glazier. The wording below the figures asks us to pray for the soul of William of Wykeham who founded the college.

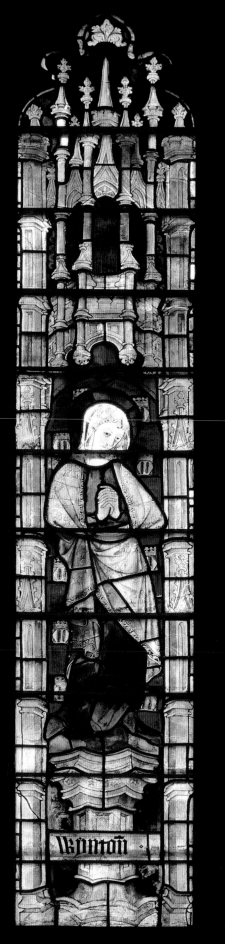

spmon ·   fundator ·   iohns rollrm

St Nicholas

This church has a fine collection of glass, much of it dating from the first half of the 14th century. Some of the later glass probably came from Stanford Hall. Over the years the glass has been moved around the church somewhat, but the present arrangement is thought to be the closest to the original distribution. The chancel windows, with their intersecting tracery, are occupied by the Twelve Apostles, set against grisaille, from *c.* 1324–30; glass from slightly later (*c.* 1330–50) can be found in the nave aisle (see, for example, St Margaret, opposite). There are numerous tracery lights with images of fish and birds as well as more conventional religious scenes – and the famous 'Gossip' panel (see p. 21). This wildlife in the tracery is sometimes accompanied by small baboon-like grotesques in the borders, which were almost a trademark of one 14th-century Midlands school of glaziers.

Above: The Crucifixion in a tracery light on the south side of the church, from the mid-14th century. *Left:* The Virgin from a Coronation of the Virgin scene, *c.* 1330.

Opposite: Two early 14th-century figures. On the left is St James ('St Iacobus') with his pilgrim's staff and bag decorated with a scallop shell; on the right is St Margaret with the dragon (her face is new, by Barley Studios). The border of cups in both panels recalls the emblem of Eleanor of Castile, the wife of Edward I.

S⁛IACORVS⁛

Stanton St John (Oxfordshire)

St John the Baptist / 13th and 14th centuries

Opposite: An unusual 13th-century scene from the medieval legend of the funeral of the Virgin. A Jew was believed to have tried to overturn the coffin but his hands stuck to the wood until St Peter made the sign of the cross and the Jew fell to the ground. He appears twice in the scene – stuck and falling. *Above:* A fine 14th-century roundel of a man scaring the birds away from his vines, probably from a cycle of the Labours of the Months. *Right:* Geometric grisaille with painted naturalistic foliage painted from the 13th century; the coats of arms were inset later.

69

Stratford-upon-Avon (Warwickshire)

Holy Trinity / 15th century

Above: Angels look down on the congregation, just round the corner from Shakespeare's grave. They show how simple painting and yellow stain can produce work of great charm. These angels would probably have originally witnessed a scene such as the Deposition, the Entombment, or even the Ascension.

Tattershall (Lincolnshire)

Holy Trinity / c. 1481–3

Right: This astonishing window is actually an assembly of the highest quality glass from various parts of the church. Among the many scenes can be seen some of the Seven Sacraments and the Acts of Mercy, angels, apostles and various coats of arms and decorative devices. Some of the panels may be by artists who also worked at Malvern Priory (Twygge and Wodshawe). Other panels were removed from the church in the 18th century and sent to Stamford and Burghley House.

Thenford (Northamptonshire)

St Mary / 15th century

Above: This small church dates from the early 13th century, but the only remaining stained glass is of the late 14th/early 15th centuries. The exquisite remains of the panel of St Christopher crossing the river with flowering staff and carrying the Christ Child have, unusually, been reset in clear glass, inadvertently giving the scene a setting in the natural world. Fish can be seen in the river and a tree on the river bank. The glass is possibly by Thomas Glazier of Oxford.

Warwick (Warwickshire)

St Mary / 1440–62

Left: The superb glass in the east window of the Beauchamp Chapel was painted by John Prudde. The large figures in the upper row are St Thomas Becket, St Alban, St Elizabeth, Isaiah, the Virgin Mary, St Winifred and St John of Bridlington. Below, centre, is the donor Richard Beauchamp (now seen with his daughter's head!), flanked by Christ and the Virgin, both with divine light radiating down. In the tracery lights above are angels with musical scores and the words of the 'Gloria' and 'Ave Regina'.

Yarnton (Oxfordshire)

St Bartholomew / 15th century

Below: We cannot be sure how much of the glass in this church is original to the building since most of the panels were given by Alderman Fletcher in the early 19th century. Some of the glass is Continental, but this fine angel, covered with feathers – some of which are peacock's – is probably English.

East Anglia

THE NORWICH 'SCHOOL' of glass painters that emerged in the 15th century with its magnificent painting clearly produced many fine windows, a few of which, thankfully, have survived more or less intact (notably at East Harling). If the 'Parliamentary Visitor' Dowsing and his colleagues had not been so efficient in their vandalism doubtless many more would still exist for us to see. Instead, many of the churches in the region are now either completely bare or house restored fragments – or, if they are lucky, have some intact tracery lights, high up and out of reach of the vandals. Nevertheless, at Long Melford we can still appreciate a fine collection of panels depicting the benefactors of the church, the local gentry and their inter-family relationships. The accuracy with which they are portrayed acts as a valuable record of the costumes, armour, headdresses and hairstyles of the times.

Other fine remains from the 15th century can be found at Salle, Saxlingham Nethergate, Bale, Cley, Combs, Ketteringham, Martham, Mulbarton, North Tuddenham, Warham, Wigginhall and Wighton. Earlier works are rarer, though some 14th-century and even earlier glass can be found at Drinkstone, Great Bricet, Mileham, Kimberley, Pulham and Saxlingham Nethergate.

The highlight of 16th-century glass in the region is without question King's College Chapel in Cambridge. The Norwich school has here been totally eclipsed by Continental glaziers with their Renaissance tastes and painterly style. At Gipping are windows of the same era by English (Westminster) glaziers attempting to keep up with current fashions.

The north side of King's College Chapel, Cambridge, first half of the 16th century.

King's College Chapel

The chapel at King's College spans two artistic periods, since while the building is late Perpendicular, the glass is decidedly Renaissance influenced. Work on the glazing began in 1515 under the guidance of the German Barnard Flower (who at the same time was probably finishing the glass at Fairford). The designer was probably Adrian van den Houte of Mechlin, while the work of certain other individuals – such as the artist Dirk Vellert – can also be detected. Work slowed after Flower's death in 1517, and it was not until the contract of 1526 that the requirements of the remaining 22 windows were specified. All but the west window (which was not filled until the 19th century) were completed by 1544. Artists of this second wave included Galyon Hone, Francis Williamson and James Nicholson (all from the Low Countries) and the English-born Richard Bond, Simon Symondes and Thomas Reve.

Each of the side windows has ten main lights and is some 11 metres (36 feet) high. They are divided into two tiers, each with four main sections as well as a so-called 'Messenger' panel containing two messengers carrying Biblical quotations. The east window is even larger. The subjects run from the childhood of Mary at the west end of the north side, via the Crucifixion in the east window to the post-Passion scenes on the south side culminating with the Assumption of the Virgin at the west end. However, Old Testament 'antetype' scenes that prefigure the New are intermingled throughout.

Above: The Virgin Mary and the Unicorn, as depicted in Flemish or Rhenish glass, from *c.* 1530. It was imported into the Memorial side chapel at King's in the 20th century.

Left: The lower half of a window on the north side from *c.* 1530. In the left-hand pair of lancets is Christ before Caiaphas; in the right-hand pair is Christ before Herod. Vellert's hand can be seen in the left pair – in the words of Hilary Wayment, his work is characterized by 'unfailing warmth as well as [an] outstanding sense of colour harmony'. In the central lancet we see two of the 'messengers' holding banderoles, one is whom is an angel.

Left: The east window, *c.* 1540. The Passion fills the upper half of the window as a single painterly scene, while the events of Holy Week occupy the lower half. Christ on the Cross is after a woodcut by Albrecht Dürer. *Above:* The door of Hell defended by devils above the Harrowing of Hell scene in one of the windows on the south side, from *c.* 1530. As at Fairford there is much interest in the nature and appearance of devils.

East Harling (Norfolk)

St Peter and St Paul / c. 1480

The glass in the east window of East Harling parish church is deservedly famous for its quality. It was preserved from the Puritans by removing it and hiding it in the attic of the local manor. Each scene is framed by holly leaf curled around a pole – almost a trademark of the Norwich school of glass painters. The subject of the window is the life of the Virgin and it features scenes from the Nativity and Passion of Christ. Above we see the Annunciation (when Christ was conceived) and right is the Visitation with St Elizabeth who was pregnant with John the Baptist (who was to 'prepare the way' for Christ). The window was given by the Wingfield and Chamberlain families.

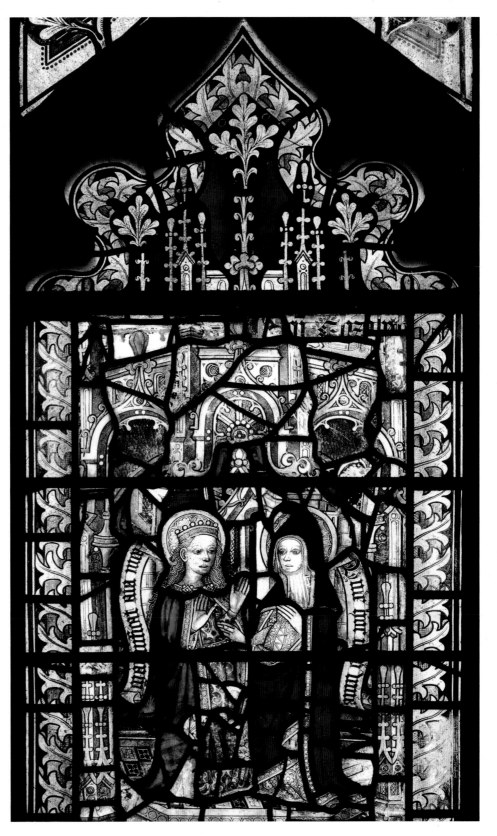

Ely Cathedral and Stained Glass Museum

Ely Cathedral, the burial place of many Anglo-Saxon kings and queens, lost nearly all of its medieval glass in the Reformation. Some indication of what might have been there, however, is given by the remains of the canopies in the Lady Chapel. The cathedral is now home to a fine collection of 19th-century glass as well as housing the national Stained Glass Museum, located in the south triforium. This focuses mostly on English stained glass of all ages, and is particularly strong in 14th-, 15th- and 19th-century, along with 13th-century French glass. As such it complements other fine collections (notably the Victoria and Albert Museum, some of whose pieces are on display here). However, the collection also includes many recent and modern panels. Some of its highlights are shown opposite.

Opposite: One of the four surviving canopies in the Lady Chapel in the cathedral, *c.* 1340–49. Unusually, peasant figures inhabit the niches. These colourful canopies hint at the quality of the windows that would have been beneath them. Coupled with the rich colouring that clearly originally covered the walls, the windows would have contributed to a wonderfully glowing space.

Below: The donors Thomas (?) and Matilda Cele, from East Anglia, second half of the 14th century, and now in the Stained Glass Museum. Donors are generally to be found at the foot of the window, but here they were placed in a tracery light.

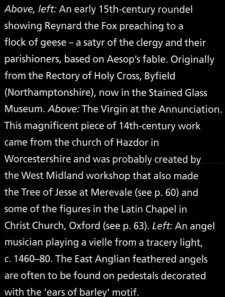

Above, left: An early 15th-century roundel showing Reynard the Fox preaching to a flock of geese – a satyr of the clergy and their parishioners, based on Aesop's fable. Originally from the Rectory of Holy Cross, Byfield (Northamptonshire), now in the Stained Glass Museum. *Above:* The Virgin at the Annunciation. This magnificent piece of 14th-century work came from the church of Hazdor in Worcestershire and was probably created by the West Midland workshop that also made the Tree of Jesse at Merevale (see p. 60) and some of the figures in the Latin Chapel in Christ Church, Oxford (see p. 63). *Left:* An angel musician playing a vielle from a tracery light, *c.* 1460–80. The East Anglian feathered angels are often to be found on pedestals decorated with the 'ears of barley' motif.

Hengrave (Suffolk)

Hengrave Hall Chapel / Early 16th century

Hengrave Hall offers an unusual example of fine stained glass surviving in a private setting. The glass was probably ordered from Troyes, France, by Sir Thomas Kytson. The overall theme spans the Creation to the Passion to Last Judgment.

Left: The Resurrection, with Christ emerging from the grave while the soldiers sleep; in the background Christ can also be seen visiting souls in Hell, which is portrayed as a huge gaping mouth. *Above:* A scene from the Last Judgment in which two apostles accompany the souls of the saved.

Leverington (Cambridgeshire)

St Leonard / 15th century

Right: The Tree of Jesse in Leverington church is one of the more unusual varieties. The 61 figures do not obviously seem to be attached to a tree and are assembled in the Perpendicular tracery without the usual sense of focusing on Christ via the Virgin Mary. Nevertheless the ensemble of figures – some old, others repaired, many completely replaced – is a splendid sight. Here we see details of King Solomon, King David and two prophets holding quotations from their prophecies.

Long Melford (Suffolk)

Holy Trinity / Late 15th century

This church has eight windows on the north side
that contain reset pieces of 15th-century glass.
Left: Figures of local gentry, particularly the Cloptons,
together with their friends and relations. We know
from records that John Clopton was a wealthy clothier
and sheriff of Norfolk and Suffolk in 1452–3, which
helps us to date the window. *Below:* A detail from
another of the windows, showing the Pietà. The
wounds from the flagellation before the Crucifixion
are strangely patterned on Christ's body. *Opposite:*
A portrait of Elizabeth Tilney, Countess of Suffolk.

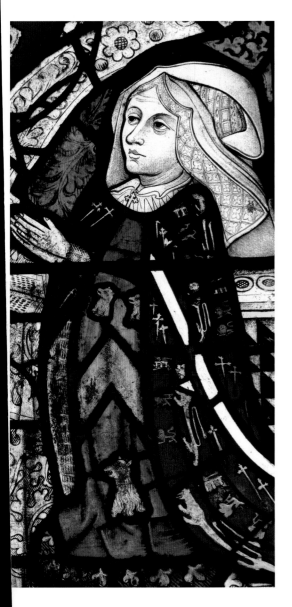

Margaretting (Essex)

St Margaret / c. 1460

Right: The fine Tree of Jesse at Margaretting is said to be by John Prudde (of Beauchamp Chapel fame). The giant recumbent figure of Jesse is at the lower centre, while the kings of Christ's ancestry occupy the central lights and the prophets who foretold his coming are in the side lights.

St Peter Mancroft

Norwich had been a centre of stained glass window production since the early 13th century, but came into its own in the 14th century and particularly in the 15th. Work of the so-called Norwich school can be seen in a number of places in Norfolk and beyond. But nowhere does such a large display of their work survive as at the huge church of St Peter Mancroft in the centre of the city, where the east window contains a magnificent collection of panels reminiscent of those at East Harling (see p. 79). They were assembled here in the 17th century from other parts of the church after a gunpowder explosion during the Puritan riots in 1648 wrecked much of the glass. The scenes are a mixture of the childhood of Christ, the funeral of the Virgin Mary and the life of St John, together with other panels of saints; the middle four panels of the central lancet and the central three panels of the bottom row are Victorian replacements.

Above: The Annunciation, with characteristic Norfolk school holly leaf around a pole.
Right: Herod giving out orders for the Massacre of the Holy Innocents, which the soldiers then carry out. In the lower right corner the clever use of yellow stain on blue grass gives a green bank with blue flowers.

Opposite: The east window. Numbering left to right and top to bottom, the scenes are a mixture of the Passion (24, 26, 38, 40); the childhood of Christ (22, 29, 30, 31, 33, 34, 35); the funeral of the Virgin Mary (27, 28); scenes from the lives of St John and St Peter (3, 6, 7, 14, 15, 16, 17, 19, 20, 21); together with panels of St Cecilia (1), St Francis receiving the stigmata (5), St Stephen (9), St Elizabeth of Hungary (10), St Catherine (12), St Faith (13). Also there is a Trinity shield (4) and donors Garnysh, Ramsey (36, 41, 42), Thomas and Margaret of Ely (37).

Above: A rare depiction, in panel 28 of the east window, of the incident in the apocryphal account of the funeral of the Virgin where a Jew was supposed to have tried to overturn Mary's coffin but found his hands stuck to it; only by the command of St Peter was he released. (See also the depiction of the same scene at Stanton St John, p. 68.) *Right:* The tracery lights above the east window contain a selection of saints and angels from different parts of the building. In the top left hand corner we see the Angel Gabriel from an Annunciation, next to God from a Coronation of the Virgin; to the right of them are Archbishop William of York and the bishop St Erkenwald (a prince of East Anglia). Immediately beneath God is a charming depiction of St John and St James as children, while to the right of this is a scene of St Anne teaching the Virgin to read (in two panels). Other figures include a sainted king with a sword.

Saxlingham Nethergate (Norfolk)

St Mary the Virgin / 14th and 15th centuries

This church has several interesting pieces from the
13th to 15th centuries. *Below left:* In this fragment
Edward the Confessor carries his emblem, a ring; the
bottom half of the figure may have been taken from
a St Christopher panel, since we see a hand clasping
a staff. *Below:* A detail of St Jerome, hard at work at
his desk translating the Bible.

The South and South-West

THE HIGHLIGHT IN THE SOUTH is unquestionably Canterbury. As befits the cathedral of the principal Province of the Church in England, its glass is superb in quality and variety. However, this in no way detracts from a host of other important sites, and even within Kent we find fascinating 12th- and 13th-century grisaille windows at Brabourne and Hastingleigh and excellent glass at Selling. Moving across the region, we find significant remains at Cockayne Hatley in Bedfordshire, while at Hillesden in Buckinghamshire the St Nicholas scenes betray the influence of the Renaissance. Heading further west, Winchester College still has fine remains of late 14th-century glass by Thomas Glazier, while the 13th-century remains at Salisbury Cathedral merit attention, even if one regrets that more did not survive the 18th-century 'restoration'.

In the South-West the cathedrals of Exeter, Wells, Gloucester and Bristol, together with Tewkesbury Abbey, all have fine 14th-century glass, often of figures under exotic canopies. Good glass of this age can also be found in smaller churches such as Eaton Bishop, Madley and Bere Ferrers. In the following century a West Country 'school' can be detected at a number of places in Dorset, Wiltshire, Somerset and Devon, including the countryside church of Melbury Bubb. Devon and Cornwall 15th-century glass definitely has a more rustic feel about it, with the glaziers emerging with their own individual charm and characteristics as can be seen at Doddiscombsleigh and Kelley in Devon and St Neot, St Kew and St Winnow in Cornwall.

The Lady Chapel and retrochoir at Wells Cathedral, 14th century

Bere Ferrers (Devon)

St Andrew / First half 14th century

The donor William Ferrers, who added the transepts to this church in the 14th century, holds a model of the church to celebrate the event. His coat of arms appears below. The strapwork in the background is a kind of intermediary phase between 13th-century grisaille and the diamond-shaped quarries that became popular in the 15th century.

Canterbury Cathedral

With glass from the 12th to 20th centuries Canterbury is, along with York Minster, the most important stained glass site in England. Particularly important are the 12th- and 13th-century panels where English glaziers first showed that they were capable of matching their Continental counterparts, including the panels of Christ's ancestors that originally lined the clearstorey of the choir. These would have numbered 86, of which some 43 have survived, seven in the clearstorey and the rest divided between the south transept and the west windows. Likewise the remains of the twelve Biblical windows that dated from before 1180 have been concentrated into two windows in the north choir aisle.

Of the various 13th-century windows the finest are the eight associated with St Thomas Becket's shrine that date from the 1220s; seven of them recount miracles that were believed to have happened after the archbishop's death while the eighth depicts scenes from Thomas's life. However, the later glass is just as impressive: the north transept window or 'Royal window', despite losing many panels to the Puritans, still has many interesting figures in the tracery lights, while the portrayals of Edward IV and his family (see p. 20) are fine 15th-century work.

Above: A detail from a typological window in the east Corona, *c.* 1180, showing Jonah being thrown overboard and devoured by a whale. In the window this is paired with the lowering of Christ into the tomb, since just as Jonah will return from the fish's bowels so too will Christ be resurrected from the tomb. *Right:* One of the Miracle windows, *c.* 1220. The bottom group of nine panels relates how a plague in the household of Sir Jordan Fitzeisulf was cured when he made a thanksgiving to Thomas. In the top fifteen panels other miracles are illustrated. Some panels just below half-way up relate the story of Mad Matilda of Cologne, a woman who, having murdered her child while in a manic state, was beaten by the populace as she made her way to St Thomas's tomb. *Below:* A detail of the Matilda story, showing her collapsed at the tomb. She later gives thanks and is miraculously restored to sanity.

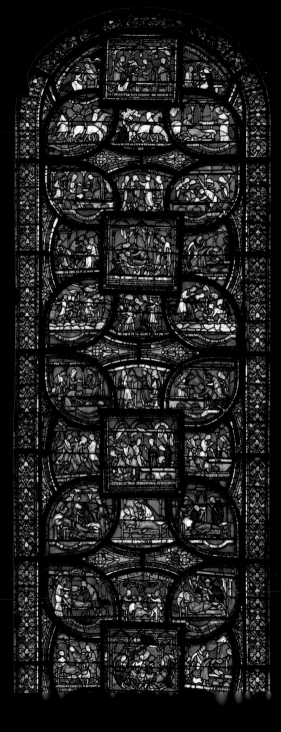

Left, above and below: This Miracle window, from *c.* 1220, depicts the curing of Gerald (or Walter of Lisors) of leprosy (above, he joyfully rides out of Canterbury afterwards), and St Thomas appearing to Eilward of Westoning in bed to heal him of blindness (below).
Right: A window, again *c.* 1220, recounting miracles relating to six people including King Louis VII, who made a pilgrimage to Becket's tomb and left a large ruby.

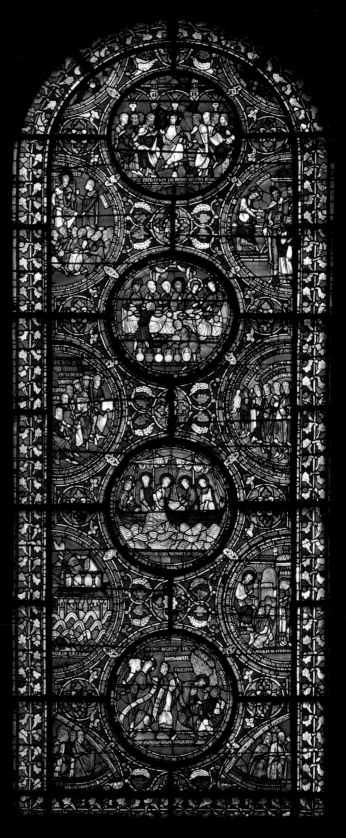

Above: In a detail of the window left, Juliana Puintel is told by Thomas to go to the shrine to be cured. *Right and below:* A typological window, from *c.* 1180, which mixes Old and New Testament scenes including Noah's Ark, Christ calling the fishermen, the Marriage at Cana and the Dispute in the Temple (a detail of which appears below). The Six Ages of the World are countered by the Six Ages of Man.

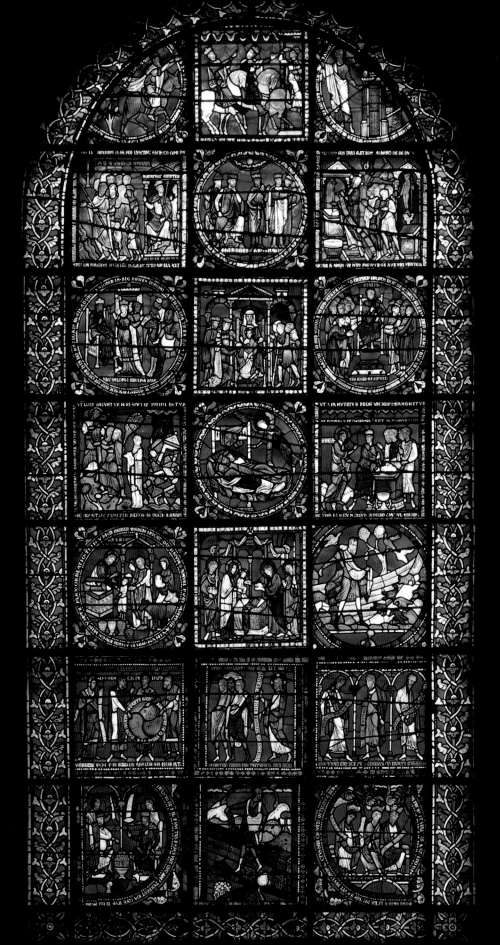

Left and above: Another typological window, with scenes from the Childhood of Christ (except the Parable of the Sower at the bottom), *c.* 1180. The typological aspect – here concerned with warning – is demonstrated by the scene of the Three Magi in bed in the centre of the window (see detail above), who are being warned by an angel of Herod's intentions; to the left Lot is warned by angels while his wife ignores the warning and is turned to stone; to the right Jereboam is warned by the prophet who in turn has been warned by an angel.

Opposite, right: The great west window at Canterbury. The lower two rows contain figures from the 12th-century genealogy of Christ, formerly in the choir clearstorey, except for the central figure of the central row (King Henry III?). In the upper half of the central row are also twelve small saints. The seven large figures of English kings above that are all that remain from the presumed 21 that filled the whole window; they are in 15th-century glass probably by John Prudde (of Warwick's Beauchamp Chapel fame). *Opposite, left above:* A detail of Aminadab from the genealogy of Christ (*c.* 1178). *Opposite, left below:* Salmon, King David's great great grandfather (late 12th century).

Cockayne Hatley (Bedfordshire)

St John the Baptist / 14th century

Above: The early 14th-century glass in this church which, architecturally, is a mixture of Decorated and Perpendicular styles, is believed to have been brought from Yorkshire in the 19th century. It includes four saints: this is a king labelled St Edward, probably meaning the Confessor.

Doddiscombsleigh (Devon)

St Michael / *c.* 1450

This church was reopened in 1879 after years of
neglect, and happily has retained very fine 15th-
century glass in five windows. The glaziers were
probably part of a school or workshop that can
also be seen working at Exeter Cathedral and
even in Somerset and Dorset. *Opposite:* The
patron of the church, St Michael, weighs souls.
Below and right: Two panels, each depicting one
of the Seven Sacraments – below is Penance, while
right is Ordination. The latter is reminiscent of the
panel in Melbury Bubb, Dorset (see p. 108).

Exeter (Devon)

Exeter Cathedral / 14th and 15th centuries

Left: The glass in the east window at Exeter was assembled from various parts of the cathedral in the 18th century. At the top are Abraham, Moses and Isaiah (all c. 1303); below them are three 15th-century figures of an angel, St Michael and St Catherine. Other figures include St Sidwell, St Helen the kings Edward Confessor and Edmund (all c. 1391). In the bottom row the central three (St Barbara, the Virgin and St Martin) are 15th century while the outer six (Margaret, Catherine and Mary Magdalene and Peter, Paul and Andrew) are from the 1303 scheme. *Below and right:* Details of Sts Peter and Paul.

Fairford (Gloucestershire)

St Mary

The church of St Mary in Fairford is rightly admired, not least because it is just about the only late medieval parish church to have survived with its glazing programme intact. The top half of the west window is mostly 19th century, but despite storms and restoration most of the other 27 windows contain a large percentage of their original glass.

The programme follows a traditional 'ideal' medieval layout, with the Old Testament subjects and characters on the north side, the New on the south, and the Crucifixion in the east window. In the west windows are the Last Judgment framed by two other 'judgment' windows. More unusual are the 'Enemies of the Church' inspired by devils high up on the north side of the nave. These include Judas, Annas, Caiaphas, Herod Agrippa and Nero. Facing them on the south side are angels who are enlightening martyrs and confessors of the faith.

The windows were initially created under the guidance of Sir John Savile from 1500 until his death in 1505. The chief glazier, however, was almost certainly Barnard Flower, the King's Glazier, who had his workshop in Westminster. He directed a team of glaziers at Fairford between 1500 and 1517 – as many as twenty different hands have been detected, six on the east window alone. In 1515 Flower went to work at King's College Cambridge where he died in 1517.

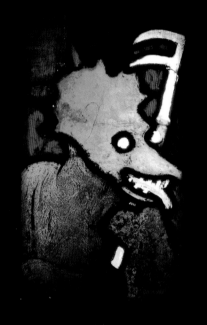

Above: Two demons above the 'Enemies of the Church' in the clearstorey windows on the north side of the building. Demons come in all shapes and colours at Fairford!

Opposite, left: One of the 'Enemies of the Church' (thought to be the Emperor Maxentius) with the head of a saint on his pike.
Opposite, right: This Crucifixion scene with Christ between two thieves in the east window is typical of the period. (A more elaborate version can be seen at King's College Cambridge, p. 78.) Around the foot of the Cross we see the traditional figures of Mary and John, the soldiers – some on horseback – and Pilate. In the lower half are scenes from Passion Week: the entry into Jerusalem, Christ in Gethsemene, Pilate washing his hands, the scourging and the Via Crucis.

Assumption in the east window of the north aisle. In the two left-hand lancets is the Flight into Egypt, with the Massacre of the Holy Innocents in the background; on the right Christ disputes with the Doctors in the Temple. Between them the Virgin Mary is carried aloft on a crescent moon. *Below and right:* Details from the Last Judgment in the west window, with souls being hounded by grotesque devils into hell and Satan with a green fish-like head and a body like a head with penetrating eyes and a mouthful of fearsome teeth.

Gloucester (Gloucestershire)
Gloucester Cathedral / Mid-14th century

Left: The vast east window at Gloucester has a
highly distinctive blue, red and white colour scheme.
Here we see two figures of apostles from this window
(St Peter, as the first Pope, holds a church), drawn
with the characteristic 14th-century S-shaped sway;
owing to the size of the window, many of the figures
reused the cartoon designs. *Above:* The head of a
king, perhaps originally from a Tree of Jesse, which
is now part of the east window of the Lady Chapel.

Hillesden (Buckinghamshire)
All Saints / Early 16th century

The highlight at Hillesden is the east window in
the south chapel where the four windows are filled
with eight scenes from stories associated with St
Nicholas. *Opposite, left:* The devil disguised as a
pilgrim strangles a boy who has offered him food on
St Nicholas's Day. Prayers to the saint subsequently
revive him. *Opposite, right:* The son of a
merchantman carrying a cup as an offering to
St Nicholas falls into the sea. He reappears when
his father offers a second cup to the saint.

Kelley (Devon)

St Mary / 15th century

Left: Although the chancel of this medieval church was refurbished in the 18th century, the east window with its Crucifixion scene has survived, albeit with some restoration. This figure is St John, looking up to the cross, and always to be found to the right in Crucifixion scenes.

Melbury Bubb (Dorset)

St Mary / Late 15th century

Below: This panel is the sole survivor in this church of a series depicting the Seven Sacraments. It shows the taking of holy orders, with a bishop blessing the tonsured novices. The style, and particularly the faces, are similar to the Sacrament panels at Crudwell in Wiltshire and Doddiscombsleigh in Devon (see p. 99).

Orchardleigh (Somerset)

St Mary / First half 15th century

Below: The remote church of Orchardleigh has a number of angels all playing identifiable contemporary musical instruments, beautifully painted in 15th-century glass. The church also has a number of the Twelve Apostles in glass of the same age, carrying screed scrolls, somewhat restored, but very fine nevertheless.

St Kew (Cornwall)

St James / c. 1469

Below: This scene, of Christ washing the disciples' feet, forms part of a Passion sequence in the east window on the north side of the church that has mercifully survived the centuries. There are also some remains of a Tree of Jesse in the church.

St Neot (Cornwall)

St Neot / c. 1500

This church has fifteen late medieval windows, which, although extensively restored in the 19th century, have retained much of their original glass. *Left:* The Creation window, which tells the Genesis story. The sequence starts at the top and reads left to right: the Creation and Adam and Eve take up the first nine panels, then there are four concerned with Cain and Abel, then the death of Adam and finally God ordering Noah to build the ark – Noah politely raises his hat to the Lord! *Above:* An angel casts Adam and Eve out of Paradise. *Opposite, left:* A detail of the Bosom of Abraham as a sheet holding the souls of the saved, from a window on the north side. *Opposite, right:* Another detail from the Creation window, of Noah's Ark with the dove released to look for land.

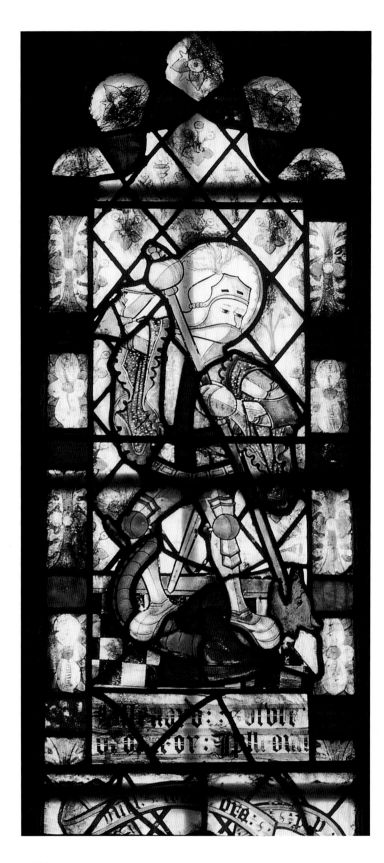

St Winnow (Cornwall)

St Winnow / Mid-15th century

This famous church in its beautiful setting with its Norman transept arch still retains some of its later medieval glass. *Left:* In the south-east window St George can be seen killing the dragon. *Below:* A saint bishop. The backgrounds in both windows are made of diamond-shaped quarries, each containing a decorative motif, sometimes from nature or sometimes even with a little scene.

Selling (Kent)

St Mary the Virgin / c. 1308

Below: Using a then fashionable device of coloured panels set against grisaille, this window features (left to right) St John, St Mary Magdalene, the Virgin and Child, St Margaret, and St John Baptist. The coats of arms show how the local dignitary Gilbert de Clare related to the king – his second wife was a daughter of Edward I. *Right, above and below:* Details of St John the Baptist and the royal coat of arms.

Tewkesbury (Gloucestershire)

Tewkesbury Abbey / First half 14th century

The abbey has an excellent collection of 14th-century glass, including the famous knights in armour that join the more familiar religious figures in the clearstorey. *Left:* Two of the knights on the north side, Hugh Despenser and Robert Fitzhamon, displaying their heraldry on their armour. Robert was the founder of the Abbey and Hugh was the first husband of Eleanor de Clare and the favourite of Edward II; he was executed in 1326. Eleanor did much work for the Abbey and most of the other knightly figures in the clearstorey are related to her. *Above:* Prophets and kings in the high clearstorey windows of the chancel where a remarkable amount of glass has survived the centuries. Here three of the figures are prophets and, unusually, have haloes. From left to right they are Jeremiah, a prophet, King Solomon and Joel.

Ticehurst (East Sussex)

St Mary the Virgin / 15th century

Right: These picturesque remains are from a 'Doom' window – a variety of Last Judgment depiction that emphasized the torments of the damned. Much of the architecture of the church is 14th century, although the west window is of the following century, making it the most likely (and certainly the most traditional) original location of the Doom window.

115

Wells Cathedral

Wells Cathedral is fortunate in still having a good amount of its original glass, mostly of the 14th century. The Lady Chapel at the extreme east end of the building has something of an enchanted feeling about it, a space almost entirely illuminated by medieval glass, even if much of it is in a fragmented state. Of the five windows in the chapel, the east window is the best preserved, although it has been much restored. However, the tracery lights still have many of their original panels, mostly filled with fine heads of patriarchs, prophets, bishops and saints.

The great Tree of Jesse in the choir is flanked by a number of majestic figures in the clearstorey, the whole ensemble being of the 14th century and with notable architectural canopies at the tops of the lights. Large canopies are to be found in the windows at the east ends of the aisles atop windows that are still just about readable though much fragmented. The Chapter House has glass only in the tracery lights, where souls rise on Judgment Day.

Above: A soul rising from the grave at the Last Judgment from one of the tracery lights in the Chapter House. These resurrection scenes and some fine decorative trefoils are the sole remains of the stained glass in the Chapter House.

Left: Two patriarchs, Simeon and Zebulun, from the tracery lights on the north side of the Lady Chapel. There are a number of these heads placed into the multiple tracery lights of some of the windows in the retrochoir and Lady Chapel; some of them are drawn from the same cartoon, but all are impressive even though some are modern copies.

Opposite: St Blaise and the pope St Leo, two of the fine figures in characteristic 14th-century colours of red, green, white and yellow stain that line the choir clearstorey. These figures have been described by one stained glass scholar as 'the most noble examples of English fourteenth-century painting.'

Opposite, left: The east window of the Lady Chapel is more or less intact, albeit with a significant amount of restoration by Thomas Willement in 1845. The main figures (left to right) are Noah, Abraham, David, Isaiah and Malachi. Beneath them are Eve, the serpent (with human head), the Virgin and Child, the brazen serpent and Moses. Relevant Biblical quotations weave around each of the figures. In the tracery lights Christ appears with angels waving censers and carrying the Instruments of the Passion. The use of a blue background by Willement, however, is somewhat controversial. *Opposite, right:* The Virgin from the centre of the Tree of Jesse in the high east window of the choir. The figure is drawn with the characteristic sway or S-shape.

Left: Abraham from the Tree of Jesse. A branch from the tree weaves its way from the side shaft and spirals around the figure. *Above:* St Cuthbert from one of the nine tracery lights in the Lady Chapel (south side). The use of whole heads to fill the tracery lights is unusual, although it is certainly popular here at Wells.

Westham (East Sussex)

St Mary / 15th century

The east window at Westham has a complete series of apostles (plus St Paul) in fine 15th-century glass – here we see St Paul, St Bartholomew and St James in the tracery lights. Each apostle carries an emblem or symbol by which he can easily be recognized: St Paul carries the sword with which he was killed, St Bartholomew a book and the knife with which he was flayed, and St James the pilgrim staff, bag and hat. The plinth of the latter shows perspective, and their very individual characterizations give them great charm.

Westwell (Kent)

St Mary / c. 1220

Right: The 13th-century Tree of Jesse at Westwell is one of the most impressive to have survived, even if the bottom two panels are 19th-century additions. Christ appears at the top; the figure beneath him (see the detail *below*) is usually the Virgin Mary, the last in line of descent, but here is somewhat puzzling for although the face is somewhat feminine the pose of the figure is more in keeping with one of the kings in the tree. Prophets at the side foretell Christ's coming while the dove of the Holy Spirit symbolizes the descent of the Spirit into the Incarnation.

Winchester (Hampshire)

Winchester Cathedral / 14th and 15th centuries

The impressive Perpendicular west window of Winchester Cathedral was destroyed in the Civil War, and today is filled with fragments which add a shimmer of light to the nave. This window must have been breathtaking when first installed and would have ranked alongside the great east and west windows at York Minster and Gloucester Cathedral. The reassembled fragments suggest that the original composition would have contained figures under canopies – high up on the left side of the window there is one opening that gives a good idea.

Winchester (Hampshire)

Winchester College Chapel / 1390s

Winchester College and its chapel were built by
William of Wykeham, who also founded New
College, Oxford (see pp. 64–5). Thomas Glazier
was employed to provide the stained glass at both
places. (His son, John Glazier, may have been the
master who glazed All Souls College, Oxford.)
The glass was removed in the 19th century from
the chapel's east window and replaced by imitation
panels, but some of the original panels were
reassembled in this window in the Thurbern Chantry.
Right: A detail of the prophet Nathan from the Tree
of Jesse by Thomas Glazier. *Above:* A Virgin and
Child, also by Glazier, also in the Thurbern Chantry.

Glossary of Stained Glass and Architectural Terms

abrasion A technique whereby flashed glass (*see* flashing) is rubbed or scraped to remove the top layer (typically *ruby*) from its white base, to allow red and white areas to appear on the same piece of glass. See p. 12 for an example, and p. 88 where the white base has been *yellow stained*.

acanthus A stylized leaf design that is thick and scalloped, found especially in *Perpendicular tracery lights*.

armature A large frame, almost always of iron, that helps support the individual stained glass panels. Typically it forms geometric shapes that are also used to give definition to the window's design, and it is found particularly in the Romanesque and early Gothic periods.

back-painting Painting on the exterior surface of the glass, to give a three-dimensional effect.

cames *See* leading.

canopy An architectural arrangement or 'niche' over or around a figure or scene. Canopies vary over time, but were particularly popular in the 14th and 15th centuries.

cartoon The full-sized drawing of the intended window showing lead lines; it was used to cut the pieces of glass to the desired shape.

chancel The eastern end of the church; it abuts the *choir*.

choir The part of the church between the *crossing* and the altar at the east end.

cinquefoil An opening in stone formed by five cusps surrounding a central circle.

clearstorey (or clerestory) The upper part of the elevation of a church, always glazed, stretching between the triforium (or arcade) and the vault. Stained glass in the clearstorey tends to be bolder in design, because of the distance from the viewer on the ground.

corrosion Generally a pitting or flaking of the surface of the glass, brought about by bad firing, the presence of potash in the glass or other impurities, and accelerated by modern pollution.

crocket A pinnacle, gable or other projection on the side of a spire or *canopy*, whether in sculpture or in painting.

crossing The place in the church where the *nave*, *transepts* and *choir* intersect.

crown glass Rather than being blown into a cylinder that is then cut and laid out flat, crown glass is spun into a disc.

Decorated The term used to describe a style of architecture prevalent in England between *c.* 1290 and *c.* 1380. Followed by the *Perpendicular*.

diaper A geometric pattern of small squares and lozenges.

finial The pointed top piece of a *canopy*, designed to emphasize the apex.

flashing The process whereby a layer of coloured glass (almost always red, or *ruby*) is added to the base layer of white, by dipping the bulb of white glass into molten red glass; as the bulb is blown the red glass adheres as a thin film. The process may be repeated to add density of colour. It was normally used to create a lighter shade of red, since *ruby* glass alone tends to be rather opaque. The same technique can be performed with other colours, but this was rarely done in the medieval period. The flashed glass might then be subjected to *abrasion*.

grisaille Clear glass, often painted with a monochrome foliage pattern, usually geometric and sometimes interspersed with small coloured pieces of glass. See pp. 13, 14 and 113 for examples.

grozing iron A piece of iron with a notch cut into it that enables glass to be trimmed to shape.

lancet A long slender window terminating in a pointed arch. This is a very common form in Gothic architecture.

leading Milled lead with an 'H'-shaped cross-section that is used to hold the pieces of glass in a window together. The strips of lead are called 'cames'.

light Any opening between *mullions* or in *tracery*.

mandorla An oval shape generated by two intersecting curves within which holy figures (usually Christ or the Virgin Mary) are placed. Typically mandorlas have radiating beams or waves.

medallion A group of panels linked by a narrative sequence within one *light*.

mouchette A curved, dagger-shaped opening in *tracery*, characteristic of the *Decorated* period.

muff The glass while it is molten in the crucible.

mullion The vertical stone shaft that divides a window into *lights*. These proliferate particularly in the *Perpendicular* style.

murrey A pink-brown colour applied to glass, introduced in the late 14th century.

nave The main body of the church between the west end and the *choir*.

nimbus A bright disc, aureole or halo surrounding the head of a saint.

Passion shield A shield with emblems of the Passion – nails, hammer, cross, etc.

Perpendicular A style of architecture popular in England from *c.* 1380 to 1530. One of the highpoints of late Perpendicular architecture is King's College Chapel, Cambridge.

pot-metal glass Glass that is coloured equally throughout its mass, so called since it is coloured in the pot, or crucible, with metals.

quarry A small, usually diamond-shaped, piece of glass individually painted, fired and leaded with other quarries to form a field, often as a background to figures. Quarries probably evolved from geometric *grisaille* as an easier and more convenient way of filling in large windows cheaply and quickly. Some are nevertheless exquisitely painted with birds, flowers, leaves, initials, symbols and rebuses.

quatrefoil An opening generated by four symmetrically meeting cusps.

rose window A large, circular window typically (though not always) divided radially by the *tracery*. It is sometimes also called a wheel window.

roundel A circular piece of glass, usually of a single colour; roundels were particularly common from the *Perpendicular* period onwards, when they are typically found painted with scenes in dark pigment and *yellow stain*; later examples may also be coloured with enamel paints.

ruby The name given to red glass.

saddle bar A horizontal metal bar to which a leaded light is fixed; it helps to prevent the glass from bowing, warping or blowing in or out.

scratching out Selectively removing part of a wash of paint by scratching, often with the wrong end of a brush.

silver stain *See* yellow stain.

strapwork Decoration consisting of an interlacing network of bands. See p. 92 for an example.

streaky glass *Ruby* glass subjected to *flashing* is sometimes uneven in its colour due to the varying thickness of the layer of red; the effect imparts a streakiness to the glass. See p. 9 and the canopy on p. 106 for examples.

tracery The patterned stonework at the head of a window, often forming ornate patterns and creating *lights* of unusual shapes. It can account for up to half of the height of the window.

transom A major horizontal division of the window part way up, found especially in *Perpendicular* windows.

vesica Similar to a *mandorla* but with a sharp intersection of the curves.

vidimus From the Latin meaning 'we have seen', the *vidimus* showed the overall design of a window and was presented to the commissioner for approval. When approved, the artist would make a full-size *cartoon*.

yellow stain A technique involving the painting of a compound of silver onto selected areas of the surface of the glass and then firing it at a particular temperature, with the result that the painted areas turn yellow. In fact the coloration actually impregnates the surface of the glass, making this a genuine staining technique (in contrast to most glass painting, which is only on the surface). The final coloration depends on the precise temperature of the firing, the strength of the solution and the number of applications. Because of the material used, this technique is also sometimes called 'silver stain'. First used in the early 14th century, it was very common from the 15th century onwards. Notable examples can be found on p. 70 (the angels), p. 108 (St John) and p. 115.

Further Reading

CVMA GB – Corpus Vitrearum Medii Aevi Great Britain
Several of the publications of the CVMA appear in the list below; a fuller list can be found on their website (www.cvma.ac.uk). This website also contains hundreds of photographs of stained glass windows from around England.

Archer, Michael, *An Introduction to English Stained Glass,* London, 1985

Baker, John, and Alfred Lammer, *English Stained Glass*, London, 1960

Brooks, Chris, and David Evans, *The Great East Window of Exeter Cathedral: A Glazing History*, Exeter, 1989

Brown, Sarah, *Stained Glass in Canterbury Cathedral*, London, 1991

——, *Stained Glass: An Illustrated History*, London, 1992

Caviness, Madeleine, *The Windows of Christ Church Cathedral, Canterbury* (CVMA GB), vol. 2, London, 1981

Cowen, Painton, *A Guide to Stained Glass in Britain*, London, 1985

——, *The Rose Window*, London and New York, 2005

Crewe, Sarah, *Stained Glass in England 1180–1540*, London, 1987

Evans, David, *A Bibliography of Stained Glass*, Cambridge, 1982

French, Thomas, *York Minster, the Great East Window* (CVMA GB Summary Catalogue 2), Oxford, 1995

——, *York Minster, the St William Window* (CVMA GB Summary Catalogue 5), Oxford, 1999

——, and David O'Connor, *York Minster: A Catalogue of Medieval Stained Glass* (CVMA GB), vol. 3, fascicule 1: *The West Windows of the Nave*, Oxford, 1987

Grodecki, Louis, *Gothic Stained Glass: 1200–1300*, London, 1985

Hebgin-Barnes, Penny, *The Medieval Stained Glass of the County of Lincolnshire* (CVMA GB Summary Catalogue 3), Oxford, 1996

Ingram-Hill, D., *The Stained Glass of Canterbury Cathedral*, Canterbury, 1960

King, David, *Stained Glass Tours around Norfolk Churches*, Norwich, 1974

——, *The Medieval Stained Glass of St Peter Mancroft, Norwich* (CVMA GB), vol. 5, Oxford, 2006

Le Couteur, John D., *English Medieval Painted Glass*, London, 1926

Lee, L., George Seddon and Francis Stephens, *Stained Glass*, London and New York, 1976

Marks, Richard, *Stained Glass in England in the Middle Ages*, London, 1993

——, *The Medieval Stained Glass of Northamptonshire* (CVMA GB Summary Catalogue 4), Oxford, 1998

Michael, M.A., *Stained Glass of Canterbury Cathedral*, London, 2004

Morgan, Nigel, *The Medieval Glass of Lincoln Cathedral* (CVMA GB Occasional Papers 3), London, 1983

Nelson, P., *Ancient Painted Glass in England, 1170–1500*, London, 1913

Newton, Peter, *The County of Oxford: A Catalogue of Medieval Stained Glass* (CVMA GB), vol. 1, London, 1981

Reyntiens, Patrick, *The Beauty of Stained Glass*, London, 1990

Rushforth, G. McNeil, *Medieval Christian Imagery*, Oxford, 1936

Wayment, Hilary, *The Windows of King's College Chapel, Cambridge* (CVMA GB, Supplementary Volume 1), London, 1972

——, *The Stained Glass of the Church of St Mary Fairford, Gloucestershire*, Society of Antiquaries of London, Occasional Papers, new series, 5, London, 1984

Westlake, N.H.J., *A History of Design in Stained Glass,* London, 1881

Woodforde, Christopher, *English Stained and Painted Glass*, Oxford, 1954

Acknowledgments

I should like to thank sincerely all those people who helped make this book possible, notably the vicars, rectors and wardens of the churches who kindly gave permission for their windows to be photographed and represented here. I would also like to thank the Deans and Chapters of the Cathedrals of Canterbury, Carlisle, Ely, Exeter, Gloucester, Hereford, Lincoln, Wells, Winchester and York Minster, as well as the Collegiate Church of St Mary, Warwick, for their permission to photograph. Photographs also appear by kind permission of the Wardens and Fellows of All Souls, Christ Church, Merton and New Colleges at Oxford and the Provost and Scholars of King's College, Cambridge.

Nor would this book be possible without the good work of scholars whose publications have brought so much information to light and I thank them for it. Any errors and omissions are entirely my own. I extend particular thanks to Tim Ayers and Sarah Brown; to all the staff at Thames & Hudson, particularly my editor Christopher Dell, the designer Geoffrey Penna and the production controller Susanna Friedman; to the many kind people who have put me up on my travels around England; and to Annick, Geraldine, my sister Caroline and her husband Mike for their invaluable support.

Index